BLUE'S CODE...

AND THE DEEP STATE

JAMES E. ABEL

This book is a work of fiction. All of the names, characters,
events and incidents in this book are a product of the author's
imagination. Any resemblance to actual persons or actual events
is purely coincidental and not intended. While certain
long-standing institutions, agencies, public buildings and
geographical locations are mentioned; the characters
and events surrounding them are wholly imaginary.

Printed in the United States of America

Published in Hellertown, PA

Cover design by Joanna Williams
Cover photos © Shutterstock

Library of Congress Control Number: 2020924306

ISBN: 978-1-950459-25-4

2 4 6 8 10 9 7 5 3 1 paperback

This book, the sequel to Side(H)arm, is dedicated to all the men and women who serve and protect law-abiding citizens. It was written in honor of the military, the police, the firefighters...and so many other professionals who put their own lives on the line every day to keep us safe...sometimes in spite of feckless politicians who would have them do just the opposite.

PROLOGUE

HEATHER WARRING, a political novice serving her first term as governor, sat at her desk in the governor's mansion in Atlanta, Georgia. There was a knock at the office door. Before Warring could react, the door opened, and a thin, 60-year-old man with short, curly, grey hair entered and asked, "Hello, Heather. How are you today?"

Warring showed deference to very few people, but this was one of the exceptions. She stood up, held out her hand, and said, "Mr. President, what an honor. I…I had no idea you were in town."

The man standing in front of her was Benjamin Ojelani, a former two-term Democratic President, who had won both of his elections in huge landslides. He smiled, shook her hand, and said, "That was intentional. I'm not here on official party business. In fact, I'm here to offer you a job in the private sector. At least that's what we will call it for the moment. And I promise you this: It's the chance of a lifetime—a chance for you to join us in remaking the world."

For the next 15 minutes, the former President explained that he, along with hundreds of others, was part of a privately funded organization with direct access to trillions of dollars, the world's most advanced technology, powerful armies and nuclear arsenals. Members included many of the world's wealthiest and most powerful people... private citizens and world leaders alike. The former President further explained that the organization's singular goal was to make the world a better place—a place where wars, sickness, famine, pollution, and social injustice would no longer exist and that members worked across continents, borders, and political parties to achieve this end.

Warring looked at the President and asked, "But why me? What do I have to offer your organization?"

He smiled and said, "What you have to offer is the use of your company."

"Warring Pharmaceuticals?"

"Yes. Although we already work with most of the world's major pharmaceutical companies, yours is different. It's privately owned. We are entering the final stages of some vital research and we need complete privacy."

"What type of research are you referring to?"

"In good time, Heather, in good time. I can't tell you that yet. But what I can tell you is that if you choose to join us, you will be provided with unlimited resources."

Warring, both flattered and intrigued, wanted to ask dozens of questions. She eyed the former President and asked, "But what about my political career? Like you, I am very ambitious and now I finally have a strong platform to achieve my long-term political goals."

The President smiled and said, "Heather, I assure you that if you accept our invitation, you will be the next President of the United States. We are very experienced at winning elections, and not just here in the United States. Good things happen to members of the Guild."

"The Guild?"

"Yes. But the very existence of our organization, even it's name, is a closely guarded secret. In fact, if any member talks to anyone about our mission or our very existence, they are immediately terminated."

"Terminated? But you just told me!"

The President laughed and said, "Then I guess you'd better join, or I'm in big trouble!"

His mood sobered, and he added, "In all seriousness, I would not be here today if I thought there was the slightest chance that you'd turn us down. You are highly intelligent, very ambitious, and brutally ruthless—when you need to be. But I do need to warn you, like Noah in the Old Testament, you are about to build us an ark—one that will take us to the final testament of the human experience. And when your work is complete, there will be world wide economic disruption, pandemics, and likely bloodshed as well. Some of it will be by design, while some of it will be an unfortunate by-product of the need for change."

CHAPTER 1

THREE YEARS LATER

A TALL, SLENDER, 25-year-old woman wearing a white hoodie, jeans, and white sneakers dodged dozens of protestors carrying *LUV Georgia* signs as she moved through the streets in the Edgewood section of Atlanta. As she peeked out from underneath the brow of her hood, her thick blond hair was visible, along with a streak of light blue hair framing one side of her face. She passed in front of a couple of eateries and bars until she reached a place on the corner with small purple lights ringing the windows and a hand-painted sign above the entrance that read "Beat Nick's." She glanced back at the protestors, opened the door, and ducked inside.

The smell of incense was immediate, and unmistakable. The one-time working-class corner bar had been repurposed into a retro hippie joint for neighborhood college kids and bohemian types. Eclectic art adorned the walls, bearing tags with the artists' names and asking prices. Lava lights illuminated the bar, and half a dozen glow in the dark peace signs were painted on the black ceiling.

The woman paused inside the door for a few seconds, pulled back the hoodie, and shook her hair into place. When she looked up, she saw three 20-something male patrons sitting together at the bar, taking those precious seconds to admire her. Her almond-shaped brown eyes were set perfectly between a thin, sculpted nose, framed by high cheekbones, and set off with an angular jaw. Her fingers were long and thin, as were her legs. Everything about her worked in perfect unison to create a beautiful yet unique look. As she was, without any makeup or nail polish, she looked like an athlete, maybe a golfer or a tennis player. Had she had been wearing full makeup and heels, she could have passed for a runway model.

When the guys realized she was on to them, they stumbled over each other's attempts at saying hello until one of them stood and asked if she'd care to join them. The bartender, a shaggy, brown-haired, 30-year-old man named Danny, looked on in amusement. He knew how it was going to end.

Danny watched as she politely declined, offered a shy smile, turned, and walked to the far end of the bar. He'd seen this pattern repeat from the first day she had showed up there three weeks earlier. She always kept to herself and quickly cut off anyone trying to strike up a conversation.

Danny moved down the bar to her and smiled. After glancing back at the men, he said, "Hey, Blue! I see you have some new admirers."

Blushing slightly, Blue said, "No, they were just being polite."

"Sure. Anyway, you're a bit early today. The usual?"

"Yeah." Pointing to the TV behind the bar, Blue asked, "Would you mind pulling up GNN?"

Danny set down a Dewar's on the rocks in front of her and said "The Guilded News Network huh? Not too many people come in here to watch the news anymore. They come in here to forget it."

"I know. Believe me, I know. But I need to watch something."

Danny turned his back, pointed a remote at the TV, and quickly found GNN. When it came on, there was some sort of political interview about to get underway. He turned back to Blue and asked, "This what you're looking for?"

"Yeah, thanks."

"Okay. Give me a yell if you need anything else," Danny said then walked back to talk with the guys at the other end of the bar.

On the television screen, the interview had just started. The man asking the questions was Brent Keaster, GNN's young lead reporter off the Atlanta news desk. His guest was Georgia's Democratic governor, Heather Warring. She was in her early fifties but didn't look it. She was a trim, five-foot-six-inches tall. Her face was unlined, and with shoulder-length black hair that held the sheen of a 30-year-old, Warring was an attractive woman, even if some credit may have been due a skilled surgeon.

But along with the looks came a palpable coldness. Warring's movements were stiff and unnatural. Her steel blue eyes didn't serve as windows to her soul; they were only used to peer into the souls of others—like laser beams through metal. Perhaps her persona was acquired, needed to maintain her standing at the top of her family owned pharmaceutical empire. Or perhaps she was just born that way, and that's what made her successful. Either way, when you were in Ms. Warring's presence, you were *supposed* to feel inferior.

As Blue sat at the bar and watched the interview, she quickly sensed there was something more going on than a simple sit-down with the governor of Georgia. While Blue wasn't into politics, she had seen the protestors outside and knew that it was not GNN's style to attack anyone on the Democratic side of the aisle. That was supposed to be Fox News's role. But at the moment, the questions being tossed her way by the GNN reporter weren't softballs. They were tough—and national in scope.

The reason for the tough interview was the confluence of two seemingly unrelated events. First, within the course of the past two months, Heather Warring had catapulted from virtual political obscurity to the odds-on favorite to become the Democratic nominee for the upcoming presidential election. While the primaries were still months away, two of the early frontrunners had recently dropped out, stating personal reasons. Both had endorsed Governor Warring.

Second, within the same timeframe, the state of Georgia had found itself ground zero of a bold, Democratic party–led program intended to enact a wide ranging package of highly restrictive state gun control laws in all Democratically controlled states.

It had all started three years earlier when the Dems had kicked off a new political strategy that its crafters privately referred to as the "Blitzkrieg." The idea was to work with all the Democratically controlled states at high speed between presidential election cycles to achieve state level gun control laws that were uniform from state to state and pushed much further than any prior laws, essentially rendering the Second Amendment meaningless. During the presidential election that year, California's legislature slipped the Limit Unnecessary Violence Act, or LUV Act as it was cleverly called, on the ballot as a referendum. It was almost too easy, being overwhelmingly approved by California's liberal voting base and quickly passed into law. Within the LUV Act were packed a number of sweeping reforms that included 60-day mandatory waiting periods for the purchase of any weapon, full background checks under the control and direction of the state's police force with unilateral authority to deny purchases to people deemed a potential threat to society, a reduction to a six-round limit that could be held in the magazine of any weapon forcing a major redesign effort onto manufacturers and instantaneously making many weapons illegal, a limit of five weapons that could be owned by any one person, a 100 percent state sales tax on any gun or gun-related purchase, and a full ban on the manufacture, sale, or use of bump stocks or any bullet specifically designed to increase mortality rates, including dum-dums and hollow-points.

The crafters of the legislation knew that many of the provisions might ultimately be thrown out in a federal court, but in the meantime, Blitzkrieg could get out in front of the federal court system, perhaps changing the culture and laws of the land—

forever.

Less than a month after California's referendum became law, similar legislation was passed in Oregon and Washington. In a tightly orchestrated move, both states, with many more to follow, saw busloads of paid activists carrying *Re-Civilize Our Streets* and *LUV US* signs at demonstrations designed to help kick-start the process.

The movement soon hopscotched across the country through Minnesota, Wisconsin, and Michigan. Then the eastern seaboard states fell like dominoes from Maine on down, all the way through North Carolina. In the end, the only eastern holdout north of the Mason-Dixon line was, surprisingly, New York.

With the Dems in control of both chambers of Congress, the Speaker of the House and the Senate Majority Leader used their bully pulpits to voice support for the new state laws while also using their leverage to steam roll over any state legislators or governors who waivered in their support.

As all of this was happening, the President, Mark Reynolds, a Republican who had won by the slimmest of margins, watched his approval ratings fall through the floor. While his Attorney General had filed all the appropriate suits, injunctions were slow in coming. The Republicans on the House and Senate floors were not getting any airtime as the media focused on the violent protest rallies being held by redneck NRA bullies.

When the first appeals case was finally decided, it came from the liberal Ninth Circuit Court of Appeals in San Francisco and was in favor of the State of California. The court based its finding on the premise that "Any state can use the police powers as provided for in the Constitution to protect their citizens from violence to the best of their ability, and that such powers include the right to restrict and monitor the possession of personal firearms by its citizenry." When the ruling flashed across the screen in the Oval Office, the man watching it knew he had just become a one-term President.

With the New York initiative temporarily held up for review by the state's court of appeals, the Dems turned their attention to Georgia as an important and "gettable" Southern state. It had a Democratic governor, half of the state's population lived within the 10 counties surrounding Democratically controlled Atlanta, and the Democrats had made significant inroads into suburbia, fueled largely by the state's booming film industry. Behind closed doors in Washington D.C., the Speaker of the House and the Senate Majority Leader both agreed that if Heather Warring wanted to be the party's nominee for President, it was her turn to step up to the plate.

And so, the Blitzkrieg had reached Georgia's doorstep. But Georgia was a far cry from the slam-dunk states of California, Washington, and most of the others where it had been passed into law. Georgians have a long-standing love affair with hunting and the right to bear arms. As soon as paid agitators carrying *Re-Civilize Our Streets* and *LUV Georgia* signs started showing up at Warring's public appearances, hunters, farmers, bikers, and NRA members started to show up to defend their Constitutional right to bear arms. For several weeks, the crowds and the tensions had risen. Finally, during a rally at the upscale Lenox Square Mall in Buckhead, Georgia, violence broke out. As the cameras rolled, ambulances took injured protestors to local hospitals while police vans carted dozens of agitators on both sides off to jail. The governor had run out of options. She would have to publicly announce her position on the proposed LUV Georgia Act.

Warring quickly agreed to an exclusive interview with GNN, but only on the condition that it be handled through their Atlanta bureau. Although she explained to the Washington D.C. GNN team that she wanted to keep it a "local affair," they knew the real reason. She wanted a political novice sitting across from her. She wanted to be in control, and she believed that Brent Keaster, the youthful face of the weekend news in Atlanta, would be punching above his weight class.

Warring's assumption proved to be wrong. Blue watched as Warring tried to bob and weave through the political minefield of questions Keaster threw at her. He repeatedly glanced down at an iPad on his lap and tried to pin her down on two key points. First, he wanted to know whether Warring believed if states had the right to impose their own gun control laws. Second, he wanted to know whether she would support the passage of the LUV ACT in her own state.

As the interview dragged on, Warring knew she was coming across as weak, and her ego wouldn't allow that to happen. When she noticed the producer pointing to an electronic clock sitting behind the camera, she saw her opening. She looked at the camera and said, "I see we are almost out of time, so in closing, let me say that as President of the United States, I will look to my Attorney General to diligently enforce all federal laws. But let me be clear. That responsibility does not equate to repealing state laws that are already on the books designed to protect the safety of its local citizenry. In the area of public safety, I view federal law as a baseline. Moreover, those laws extend beyond gun control, and they include such things as environmental safety as well. I believe it is time for the federal and state governments to work together on these issues for the benefit of our fellow citizens."

As GNN went to commercial break, Warring felt good. She had supported her party's position—without being cornered into what it implied for the state of Georgia. She had dodged a bullet.

But back at GNN headquarters in Atlanta, an animated discussion had broken out. Several phone calls were made, and a decision was relayed back to the interview team. Fifteen more minutes of interview time had just been carved out.

In a posh, private room inside a private club in Washington D.C., the Speaker of the House sat with the Senate Majority Leader. With drinks in hand, they compared notes on what they had just heard. The Speaker set down her Blanton's on the rocks, turned to her drinking partner, and asked "Did you hear that? She just told the world that as President, she'd defer to the states not only on gun laws but climate regulations as well." Laughing in advance of her own punch line, she said, "The sky really is the limit!"

The Senate Majority Leader joined the laughter and added, "Yup, a one-way street to stricter laws, while here in Washington, we stay out of harm's way. We should've thought of this years ago."

The Speaker smiled and glanced down at the iPad in her lap. She turned back to the Senate Majority Leader and said, "Okay, let's see how she does after the break. This next question is gonna force her into a corner."

At Beat Nick's, Blue watched as the interview flashed back on the screen. Warring looked relaxed, thinking there was about to be a final wrap up. But instead, Keaster, reading from his iPad, said, "Governor, there's one last question that, with all due respect, you've been ducking all night. What about Georgia? Will you or will you not support the LUV Georgia Act that is currently being debated in the state legislature? I think the people have every right to know if you are willing to help stem the tide of unnecessary violence and killings occurring every day in our great state of Georgia."

Warring's face turned to stone. She awkwardly adjusted her sitting position and stared at Keaster, boring a hole through his skull.

Why, you little piece of shit. Who the hell do you think you are?

Keaster couldn't take it. His eyes dropped. Ten seconds passed before he finally raised the courage to look at her and ask, "Governor?"

A smirk slowly crossed Warring's face. She leaned in toward him and said, "Mr. Keaster. That is how you pronounce your name, is it not? You know, the same as the body part?"

The cheap shot seemed to pump new courage into Keaster. He looked at Warring, smiled, and said, "That's right, Governor, just like the body part."

"Well, all right, then, Mr. Keaster. I'll answer your question, in spite of the discourteous manner in which it was presented."

Warring turned away from Keaster, looked directly into the camera, and said, "To all the good citizens of Georgia, the following words are for you, and you alone. Even though it has been the greatest privilege of my life to serve as your governor, my plans do not include running for a second term. Should you and the people of this great country bless me with their support, by this time next year I hope to be preparing to serve you in a new capacity, as your President. As such, I think that Mr. Keaster needs to direct his question not to me, but to the candidates wishing to succeed me as governor. In that way, it will be you, the voters in Georgia, who will decide whether the LUV Act is passed into law. For that reason and that reason alone, if the legislation currently under review in our state house should get passed and cross my desk, I promise each and every one of you that I will veto it, to protect your rights as citizens of this state to make that decision at the ballot box, rather than by a bunch of politicians in a back room. Thank you, God bless you, and good evening."

Warring gave Keaster a tight-lipped smile as she triumphantly stood up and flashed a much broader smile to the camera. With Keaster looking like a scolded puppy, the producer had no choice but to motion for the coverage team to cut to a commercial break.

Back in Washington D.C., the Speaker shook her head in anger, snapped up the remote, and turned the TV off. She looked over at the Senate Majority Leader and said, "Looks like we need to rethink our decision on our presidential nominee."

The Senate Majority Leader took a deep breath and said, "Actually, I'm not sure that what we think means a damn thing."

"Why the hell would you say that? We run this fucking town."

The Senate Majority Leader looked out of the corner of his eyes and offered a tight-lipped smile, not the kind that friends share. *No, you idiot. The Guild does. But I guess you wouldn't know that!*

The Speaker glared at him and said, "What are you smirking about?"

The Senate Majority Leader set his drink down, straightened up in his chair and said, "Didn't you hear what the lady just said? She wasn't really talking to the voters in Georgia; she was talking to all of America. And she what she just told them that their votes count, that they actually mean something. Somehow, she just managed to distance herself from our little shithole here in Washington D.C. at the very time she's running for President. I don't know about you, but that's what I call political genius."

The Speaker slammed her drink down on the table, stood up, and walked out of the room as the Senate Majority Leader watched, shaking his head from side to side. *Bitch!*

Back at the bar, Blue pulled her eyes away from the screen, mumbling under her breath "Mommy dearest." She grabbed her bar tab from the empty glass in front of her, looked at it, put down a $10 bill, and stood to leave.

Danny noticed and walked over. He picked up the 10-spot and asked, "Need change?"

"No, we're good."

Danny nodded, picked up the remote, and turned off the television. As Blue pulled up her hood, Danny asked, "So, why the interest in politics? I never would have guessed you were into that stuff."

Blue nodded and said, "Never was. Not until I met her."

"You know the governor?"

Blue instantly regretted her words and nervously said, "Uh, not really. I met her once, that's all. So anyway, gotta go." Then she walked toward the door, smiled at the three guys who once again had their eyes glued on her, and walked out. Danny was also looking at her, but not for the same reason. He was pretty sure he had just figured out who she really was.

CHAPTER 2

WHEN THE SOUNDMAN removed the battery pack from Governor Warring's lower back, she turned to one of her aides and said, "Please escort Mr. Keaster and his crew off the grounds. I have other business to attend to."

Governor Warring had started to walk out of the room when Keaster called after her and said, "Governor, I'm sincerely sorry if I said or did anything to offend you. It certainly wasn't my intention."

Warring paused, turned around, and said, "That's quite alright, Mr. Keaster. I hope things work out for you."

Keaster's broad smile quickly dimmed as he pondered the meaning of her words.

Keaster and his team had a bit of a drive ahead of them. The interview hadn't taken place inside the current governor's mansion in Atlanta. It had taken place at Georgia's original governor's mansion in Milledgeville, Georgia, which is about 100 miles southeast of Atlanta. The mansion,, built back to the late 1830s is the house from which Governor Joe Brown fled in advance of the arrival of General William T. Sherman and his Union army on their way to Savanna during the Civil War. It's also the house that Sherman later used as his campaign headquarters.

Two years earlier, Warring had made a generous offer of $40 million dollars for the temporary use of the house until the end of her term as governor. As part of the deal, Warring had agreed to pick up all incremental expenses for security and transportation back and forth to Atlanta needed in transacting the state's business. She had also agreed to pay for some long overdue repairs to the mansion. The money was of no concern to Warring. Although her tax returns were not yet public, estimates of her personal fortune went as high as $15 billion.

When Warring had first announced her desire to reside at the Milledgeville Mansion, her presidential campaign manager, Jimmy Harris, was taken completely off guard. He pulled her aside, warning her that it could be political suicide to move into the very house from which slavery had been proclaimed a white man's privilege and where so much of the confederate succession planning had taken place. But Warring loved proving her confidants wrong. She went on the offensive, proclaiming that she wanted to use the house as a platform to "denounce Georgia's role in antebellum slavery and to turn to the future, seeking to unify people of all colors and creeds in a multicolored blanket of peace, hope, and love."

With GNN's help, it worked—both from a public relations standpoint and as a smokescreen to cover up her real motive, which was to move out of the governor's mansion in Atlanta. She needed complete privacy to execute her long-term plan, and the Old Governor's Mansion in the sleepy little town of Milledgeville, Georgia, offered her a convenient solution.

After the deal was struck, Warring immediately commissioned all the agreed-to improvements in the mansion as well as some significant temporary changes of her own design. Most of them were on the lower level of the house.

That is where Heather Warring wanted to establish a war room for her run at the Presidency of the United States. But it was also where the original kitchen, used by slaves to prepare meals for Governor Joe Brown and his guests, still remained intact. So, Warring had new temporary walls inset within the outer perimeter within which she had built a high tech, highly secure war room that could later be removed.

That's where Governor Warring was now headed. She left the interview room and walked down a center hallway to a 10-by-10-foot square foyer at the back of the house. Both the hallway and the foyer were under camera surveillance, monitored 24/7 by off-site Warring Pharmaceuticals security personnel. The foyer had one exterior wall to the left of the hallway with a solid steel door that opened to the backyard. To the right of the hallway was a door leading to the family's private living quarters. Warring had never married, so it was only her and her adopted daughter, Jessie, who lived in that wing of the house.

Directly across from the center hallway was a solid wall with no windows or doors, adorned with an early painting of the mansion from the 1840s. Directly to the left of the hallway was a recently installed elevator. With an old stairway temporarily sealed off as part of Warring's changes, the elevator was the only means of access to the lower level.

When Warring reached the foyer, she turned to her left, entered the elevator, and swiped a key FOB. The door closed, and the elevator descended. The foyer on the lower level was identical in size to the one above it. But there were no doorways, windows, or surveillance cameras. It appeared to be a dead end. When Warring exited the elevator, she approached a large set of bookshelves directly across from the elevator, walked up to a small black metal box sitting on one of the shelves, and stood in front of it, moving her eye up close to the retinal scanner inside. A split second later, she heard a clicking sound and watched as the bookshelves separated, revealing a doorway into another room. She walked through it, and the bookcases closed behind her. She was now in her war room, a masterpiece of modern design, technology, and security. It was about 25 feet long and 20 feet wide with no windows. But it was well lit with LED lighting placed throughout a white, suspended ceiling. The white-panel walls were supported from behind with aluminum studs, and the flooring was a light gray industrial-style carpet.

Twelve television monitors, three on each wall, were flush-mounted using an aluminum bracing system to support them from behind. Some of the screens were streaming news from media outlets, while others were receiving feeds from strategically placed cameras throughout the mansion, and still others were currently blacked out—their specific purpose unknown. In the middle of the room was a conference table with seating for 12. Behind all the modern architecture of Warring's war room stood the old kitchen, still in its original state. The governor had built a room within a room.

Governor Warring sat at the conference table and punched a button on a large panel. A phone could be heard dialing from overhead speakers. Within seconds, one of the screens was filled with the face of Jimmy Harris, her campaign manager. He was in his mid-fifties with a shiny, shaved head, squinty eyes, and a deep Southern accent. Warring offered no greeting, instead asking, "So, who was the son of a bitch that just tried to throw me under the bus?"

Harris offered a weak smile, a nervous habit trait of his, and said, "I have it on good authority that the decision came from none other than the Speaker of the House. She wanted to test your mettle."

"Why that dried-up old prune!"

"Now, now. You still may need her help up here in D.C., whether you like it or not. Besides, the post-interview polls show that you just kicked ass. Nobody in Washington's gonna be able to stop you, not if we stay on plan. You're the fresh-faced outsider, and you were spectacular governor—truly spectacular. Sometimes I don't think you need me at all."

The flattery worked. Governor Warring was noticeably pleased with herself. She shifted direction and asked, "So, were you able to find out what's going on in New York? The LUV Act should be a piece of cake for those guys."

Jimmy grinned widely and said, "Apparently, the governor's been caught with his pants down. Quite literally."

"What do you mean?"

"Turns out, he decided to run the LUV New York Act by his court of appeals for political cover upstate. You know, so they could rubber stamp its constitutionality. Hell, there's only one conservative left on the court."

"So, what's the hold up?"

"That one conservative, a guy by the name of Jim Nichols, pulled the governor aside two weeks ago and told him that he's in possession of some very explicit conversations between the governor and not one, but two of his former romantic liaisons. And get this: One was a woman; the other was a man. The judge even played the recordings for him."

"Okay, so what does this Nichols guy want?"

"Well that's the crazy part. He doesn't want anything—at least not of monetary value. Hell, we offered him 5 million dollars, and he wouldn't take it. All he said was that if the governor jams the LUV Act through, he's gonna release the recordings to the press."

"Well, that's certainly odd."

"What do you mean?"

"How many people do you know who still believe in the Constitution but are willing to play as dirty as we do?"

Jimmy let out a deep belly laugh and said, "I hear ya, Gov! So, what do you want me to do, follow the Pennsylvania blueprint?"

"Of course, but please, no details."

"As always, Governor. As always."

"Okay, now that that's settled, all I have to do is get that insolent daughter of mine back home."

"Still MIA, huh? Isn't she scheduled to make one of her presentations next week? At Cornell if I reacall correctly."

"She is, and she will. We've located her and Travis is en route as we speak."

"Where did you find her?"

"Atlanta. Now you get back to your business, and let me handle mine."

"Roger that, Governor."

The screen went black. The governor stood up, glanced around, and walked toward the bookcases. When she passed an electrictronic eye, the bookcases opened up, and she walked out of the room.

CHAPTER 3

THREE BLOCKS NORTH of Beat Nick's, an over-weight, middle-aged man with thinning salt-and-pepper hair and the flushed complexion of a drinker shielded his face with a newspaper as Blue walked past his black BMW 750Li. She continued down the sidewalk, crossed the street, and entered a small bungalow-style home.

The house, built in the 1920s, had Arts and Crafts styling cues, including clapboard siding, gingerbread trim, a small covered porch supported by two angular white wooden pillars, and a solid oak front door. But it had not yet been restored to its former glory. Its once colorful trim paint was faded and peeling, some of the wood showed signs of rot, and the lawn was full of weeds and bare patches. It was one of several houses in the neighborhood owned by slumlords who used them as a source of easy cash from the college kids and artist types attracted to this section of Atlanta.

When Blue disappeared inside, the man in the BMW tossed his newspaper aside, opened the car door, and stepped out onto the street. He hitched up his pants, glanced around, and pulled his overcoat closed, careful to make sure his shoulder holster and the .38 special it held were hidden from sight.

Inside the house, Blue took off her hoodie and

hung it on a hook by the front door. She paused in the small entryway, listening for signs of life. She glanced up the steps and called out, "Hey, Peanut, you up there?"

Blue heard a thin, frail voice say, "Yup. Be down in a minute."

"Okay, take your time. I'll see what we can do about dinner." Then, Blue walked down the narrow center hallway and into the kitchen.

The kitchen needed an upgrade. It still had its original cast-iron sink and wooden cabinets that had been painted far too many times by people in too much of a hurry to remove the hinges. Its 70s-era drop-ceiling hid the sagging plaster ceiling above. The faded, green linoleum on the floor dated to the late fifties, was ripped in spots, and pulled up from the plywood underlay where moisture had seeped in from the crawl space under the house.Blue walked up to the fridge, opened the door, and peered inside. Twenty seconds later, she pulled out an Arby's bag from behind an aluminum covered casserole dish and triumphantly called out, "Hey, we're in luck. We still have some roast beef sandwiches from the other d—"She never finished the sentence. When she turned around, she found herself face-to-face with the man who, minutes earlier, had been sitting in the BMW. He was blocking Blue's escape, and his coat was now open, revealing his shoulder holster and gun. But Blue didn't panic or scream. She casually set the Arby's bag on the table, smiled, and said, "Travis. You found me."

He returned the smile and replied, "You knew I would."

"Yeah. I guess so." Then, Blue walked up to Travis, and they shared a quick hug.

Travis pulled back."So, then you know why I'm here."

"Of course. But I am an adult, and she can't run my life forever."

"Ha! Good luck with that. I've been trying to leave her for the past 15 years."

"But this is different. You work for her; I don't."

"Don't you? Seems like she pretty much tells both of us what to do and when to do it."

"That's my point. I'm sick and tired of being manipulated. Besides, I saw some things back at the house that…"

Travis held up his arms and said, "Stop. I don't want to know. I'm just here to bring you home."

"What if I won't go with you. Then what?"

"Well, then you'll probably be reading my obit in the papers. That is, if they ever find my body."

Blue frowned and said, "Don't you dare say that! It can't be that bad."

Travis laughed and said, "Hey. Don't make me find out the hard way."

Travis looked Blue up and down said, "By the way, love the new look! Blond hair…that blue streak…jeans and sneaks. Going incognito, I take it?"

"I guess. But this is also who I really am. Out-side of Warring's World, my name is Blue. It's the name I prefer, and the only one I used up until the day she adopted me."

"Okay, Blue. Then that's what I'll call you, at least when your mom's not around."

Travis heard footsteps coming down the steps and started to reach for his gun as he asked, "Who's that?"

"Relax, it's Peanut. You remember her, don't you?"

"Oh, yeah. Peanut!" He smiled.

Peanut reached the bottom of the steps, turned the corner, and froze when she saw Travis. She was in her late teens, stood less than five feet tall, and weighed barely 100 pounds. She had thin, shoulder-length, dirty-blond hair that was pulled back with a single hair tie and thin, bird-like lips. Like a mistreated rescue dog, there was a nervous insecurity about her that couldn't be missed. Blue moved past Travis and put her arm around Peanut and said, "It's okay. You remember Travis. Don't you?"

Travis chimed in, "Yeah, you remember me!"

Peanut quietly said, "I do. You're the man who helped me."

Blue said, "That's right. And he's here to help us again. Okay?"

Peanut, who had buried her eyes in the floor, looked up, got a worried look on her face, and said, "But we don't need help now. Do we?"

Blue said, "Maybe not, but we can talk about that later."

Travis, noticing the brown Arby's bag, said, "Yeah. Let's talk about that later. Right now, it looks like you guys were getting ready for dinner, so how about if I take both of you beautiful young ladies out. You name the place. I'm buying!"

A smile crossed Peanut's lips and, glancing at Blue, she said, "I love the hot dogs at The Varsity."

Blue smiled and gave Travis a nod. Travis said, "Okay. Then The Varsity it is. Let's go."

Blue looked at Peanut and said, "Since we're going out, why don't you run upstairs and put on those new jeans I got you the other day. I think they look so cool on you."

Peanut smiled and said, "Okay. I'll be right back."

As soon as Peanut left the kitchen and walked up the steps, Travis looked at Blue and asked, "What's with her? She doesn't look so hot."

"That's why I sent her upstairs. I wanted you to know that she's fighting some kind of lymphoma."

"Sorry to hear that. Is she getting treatment?"

"Sort of. I mean she's seeing a doctor at a local clinic, but I don't think she's getting the kind of quality help she really needs. I went with her last time, and I don't know. I wasn't impressed, if you know what I mean."

"So, is that why you came here, because she was sick?"

"No. I mean, yes. I guess so. We've stayed in touch ever since she moved out of the foster home when she turned 18, but it's only been a month since she told me she was sick."

"I may be out of line here, but you need to bring her back with us. With your mom's connections, she can get her the best help in the country."

Blue nodded her head. "Yeah, I know."

Peanut could be heard coming back down the steps. Blue put her finger to her mouth and whispered, "We'll talk later."

Peanut turned the corner, and Travis held out

his arms and said, "Come on, girls, turn around, out the door! Let's go get some hotdogs. They have booze at this place, don't they?"

CHAPTER 4

INSIDE THE MASTER bedroom of a gentleman's farmhouse overlooking Oneida Lake in western New York, the alarm on Jim Nichols's cell phone went off. Judge Jim, as he liked to be called, was 74 years of age and was fighting severe arthritis, likely brought on by a lifetime of daily running, biking, and hiking. In spite of that, he looked to be in good shape and had light blue eyes and a full head of thick silver hair. He glanced over at Barbara, his wife of 52 years, saw that she was sound asleep, and quietly maneuvered his way out of bed and turned off the alarm. He showered and shaved, put on an old pair of khakis and a golf shirt, and pulled on some slip-on shoes. He figured at the age of 74, what he wore under his judge's robe was his own damn business.

The judge had to be 120 miles away in Albany by 10:00 a.m., when the New York states Court of Appeals, the highest court in the state, was going into session to hear the opening arguments regarding the constitutionality of the New York LUV Act. Judge Jim, as he liked to be called, was the last remaining conservative on the court, a consequence of New York law whereby the governor fills vacancies for the 14-year terms, and New York hadn't seen a Republican governor since 2006.

After a quick breakfast of bacon, eggs, and orange juice, the judge glanced out the window and saw a black limo pull into his driveway. Up until the past year, he had always insisted on making the drive himself. But after several minor fender benders and a continued deterioration in his eyesight, Barbara had convinced him to use the state-provided driving service. He walked upstairs, nudged Barbara awake, and said, "See you tonight. I'm off to the court room."

Barbara forced her eyes open, smiled, and said, "Okay, honey. Give me a call when you're on your way home."

Judge Jim nodded, said, "Will do," and headed out to the car.

When he got there, he saw an unfamiliar man holding the back door open. The man, seeing the puzzled look on the judge's face said, "Good morning, sir. I'm Frank. Anthony wasn't feeling good this morning, so they asked me to fill in. I hope that's all right with you."

The judge smiled and said, "Of course it is. Nice to meet you, Frank. Just get me there on time—without any speeding tickets."

Frank returned the smile and said, "You got it, sir." He closed the judge's door and walked around to the driver's side.

An hour later, well down the road on I-90, Frank adjusted the rearview mirror so he could see the judge and said, "By the way, there's a bottle of water in the cooler back there if you'd like. Anthony told me to take good care of you."

The judge smiled and said, "Thanks. I appreciate that." Then, the Judge reached down, opened the cooler, pulled out the ice-chilled plastic bottle, twisted off the cap, and took a drink.

****

At about the time that Judge Jim arrived in Albany, Travis pulled up in front of the house where Blue and Peanut were staying to pick them up for the ride back to Milledgeville. The night before, he had spoken to Governor Warring, and she had agreed to let him stay in Atlanta for the night.

Inside, Blue was upstairs helping Peanut pack her clothes. Pulling some jeans and T-shirts out of the small chest of drawers, she glanced at Peanut and said, "Come on, show me a smile. It's gonna be different this time. You're not going into one of my mom's foster homes. You and I are gonna be in the same house—the governor's house! And my mom promised me that she'd get you all the medical attention you need."

Peanut flashed a weak smile and said, "I know you're right, but I'm still not sure."

Blue stopped what she was doing, sat down on the bed, patted her hand next to her, and said, "Come here. Sit down."

Peanut sat down and Blue put her arm around her shoulder and said, "I know what's bothering you, and what that man did to you last year. I can't make it better. But it wasn't my mom's fault. He was just an evil man who somehow slipped through the cracks. He's long gone by now. I promise."

Peanut didn't answer. Her head dropped, and she started to cry.

Blue held her in her arms and softly said, "I know honey. I know."

An hour later, Travis and Blue were in the front seat of the BMW, 15 minutes into the 90-minute drive to Milledgeville. Peanut was sound asleep, sprawled out in the rear. During the time Blue had been staying with Peanut, she had often seen Peanut struggle to stay awake for more than a couple of hours at a time. Blue checked on Peanut and then turned to Travis and said, "Listen, I need to tell you some things… whether you want to hear them or not. It has to do with my mother."

Travis took his eyes off the road for a second, looked at Blue, and said, "Jessie—I mean Blue—please don't put me in the middle. My job is family security—period. I'm not part of your mother's political inner circle, and I don't want to be. You understand. Don't you?"

"Of course, I do. But I have to tell someone, so please, hear me out. This will stay just between you and I. I swear."

"Okay. I'm listening."

"Good. So, have you ever been allowed down into my mom's war room—the one in the basement?"

"Nope. I'm not allowed on that floor. The only way down there is that new elevator she had put in, and I don't have the security clearance to use it."

"I'm not allowed down there either. At least, not officially."

Travis cut her off, "Whoa, I don't like where this is going."

"Okay, then. I'll tell you about that some other

time. But I know you've been in the back foyer up on the main floor, just outside our living quarters."

"Of course. I make regular security rounds up there. You know that."

"Then you're familiar with that back door, where you can come in from the backyard?"

Travis nodded and said, "Sure."

"About a month ago, maybe about two in the morning, I couldn't sleep, so I walked down the hall from my bedroom and opened the door to the foyer. I was headed out to the sitting room to work on my book."

"And?"

"I saw one of mom's security team holding the back door open for someone."

"So what? That's where most of your mother's political visitors come and go. They pull around back where there's more privacy."

"I know. But what if I told you that the visitor I saw was the President of the United States, the current one?"

"What the fuck! Sorry, I mean—oh, shit. You know what I mean. There's no way. Why would the President pay a visit to the very person who's about to oust him from office? Impossible. You must have been dreaming or something, Why the hell are you telling me this anyway?"

Blue, who loved to get Travis worked up, laughed and said, "Ha! I knew that's how you'd react!."

"Well, then stop talking about it. Do yourself a favor. Forget whatever it is you saw, and never mention it to your mother. You hear me?"

Blue smiled smugly and said, "I understand. But

I've seen more than that." She gave him a poke in the arm and asked, "Wanna know what else?"

Travis started singing out loud, "La la la la, I can't hear you."

Blue laughed for a minute and then went silent. Travis refocused on his driving.

Several minutes passed before Travis said, "Listen, Blue. We go way back, you and I, and I'd do anything for you. You know that."

Blue nodded and said, "I do."

"Well, then, be careful and stay out of your mom's political life. Up until now, you've been a big asset to her. For your own sake, keep it that way. Understood?"

"Yeah. Understood."

Ten minutes of silence followed before Blue said," Why do you think she is the way she is?"

"What are you talking about? You mean her personality or what?"

"Of course. Have you ever seen her tell a joke, smile, hold a two-way conversation like a normal person? All I ever get are directives."

"Well, since you put it that way, I can't say as I have. But since you brought it up, I might be able to give you a little insight into why she is the way she is."

"Really?"

"Yeah. About 10 years ago, in fact just before she adopted you, she called me one night. It was back when she was still living at the family estate in Buckhead."

"And?"

"And she asked me to drive over to her place. She said she wanted to talk."

"Oh, this is getting good!"

"So when I got there, I could tell right away she had a few too many martini's under her belt. She makes me one, tells me to sit down, and for the next hour I had to listen to her life story."

"Go on!"

"All she did was complain about how her mother never loved her. She told me that growing up, she was the apple of her daddy's eye and because of that, her mother resented her. There she sat, a beautiful, single billionaire with the entire world by the balls, and all she could do was feel sorry for herself."

"Wow. I never knew any of that! Did she ever mention it to you again?"

"No, and thank God! I can't stand people that spend their entire lives feeling sorry for themselves."

"Understood. But it is sad, nonetheless."

"Yeah, real sad!"

A half-hour later, they pulled into the driveway at the governor's mansion. Blue knew that the reunion with her adoptive mother was not going to be pleasant.

CHAPTER 5

IT WAS A beautiful, fall day on the Cornell University campus in Ithaca, New York. The leaves on the trees had turned brilliant shades of yellows and reds, and the sun had finally dried out the stubborn dew that had covered the grass all morning. Students were pouring into Bailey Hall, anxiously awaiting the arrival of Jessie Warring. This was the final stop on her speaker's tour through all the Ivy League schools and a few other top schools on the east coast, including Duke, Bucknell, and Lehigh University.

The big turnout wasn't just because she was the daughter of Heather Warring. Jessie had built quite a following as the national poster child for all that could be accomplished when underprivileged kids, especially women, were given a fair shake in society. While the marketing was subtle, the speaking tour was designed to showcase Governor Warring's strong commitment in this area by reminding potential voters about her charitable foundation— Warring's Women of America. The WWA, as it was generally referred to, had been established and funded with Warring family money. Its mission was to ensure that underprivileged young women throughout America would have access to the same general living and academic standards as were available to the wealthy.

The backbone of the WWA was a national network of foster homes, each equipped with state-of-the art educational programs, instructors, nutritional programs, and initiatives focused on building self-esteem. Over the years, WWA had developed close ties to many local governments and other charitable organizations to help identify young girls who could be helped.

For the past five years, Heather Warring had tirelessly focused media attention on all the good that WWA had accomplished, and she had used Jessie, her adopted daughter, as the centerpiece of the political strategy. It had become common knowledge that Jessie Warring had been plucked off the streets of Savannah as a homeless 15-year-old and had gone on to graduate from Princeton University with high honors, sit on the boards of various charities all across the country, and was about to publish a motivational book for young women.

But one of Heather Warring's most closely guarded secrets was the fact that Jessie had been very carefully pre-screened before her adoption ever took place. Warring had commissioned extensive background checks on Jessie's past, her physical health, and her mental acuity. Warring knew that Jessie's IQ was north of 145, and that she was physically healthy, very attractive, self-assured, and mature well beyond her age. Perhaps most importantly, Warring also knew that Blue had not spent years on the streets of Savannah or in various foster homes. Blue had actually spent the greater part of her young life in a stable home environment with her father who owned a small but successful restaurant and her stay-at-home mom. It was only after her mother had died of cancer, and her dad died of alcohol poisoning after drowning his sorrows in a liquor bottle that Jessie had ended up in foster care.

In reality, Jessie Warring was an extremely flawed "proof of concept" for Warring's Women of America. But Heather Warring wasn't concerned. The nation's mainstream news media was not about to rat out Heather Warring. She was the new darling of the left, and the WWA was a key foundational block in her plan to become President of the United States.

As students streamed into Bailey Hall, Molly Nichols, a 22-year-old graduate assistant in Cornell's College of Arts and Sciences, worked her way through the crowd toward her reserved seat in the second row.

Molly was a five-foot-four-inch tall strawberry blond with light blue eyes and a beautiful smile. Always full of energy, today she was in extra high gear, anxious to hear what Jessie Warring had to say. In fact, Molly was one of the event's coordinators.

As Molly took her seat, she could feel the electricity in the air. The buzz in the audience was almost deafening, perhaps aided by the high level of security that was moving into place. Men in black suits wearing earbuds were taking positions on both sides of the stage, down on the floor in front of the stage, and at all the back exits. Their presence served as a reminder that those in attendance were about to hear from the daughter of the leading presidential candidate.

As Molly settled in to her seat, the dean of students

walked to the podium and welcomed the audience. She then read off the long list of Jessie Warring's achievements, including her role as the spokesperson for the WWA, her academic credentials, the book she was working on, and the numerous charitable boards she served on. The dean ended her introductory remarks by saying, "Without further ado, I am honored to welcome to Cornell University an amazing young woman who has overcome extreme adversity and, in so doing, provides an example of how women of all socioeconomic backgrounds can become leaders in the new women-centric America that's unfolding before our very eyes. Please join me in welcoming Jessie Warring to our stage."

Applause rippled through the hall as Jessie walked out and approached the podium. She didn't look anything like the young woman who had been hanging out at Beat Nick's a week earlier. She was now wearing a $3,000 black pantsuit, a cream-colored silk blouse, and low-healed black pumps. Her hair was no longer blond with a blue streak. It was black, the color that Governor Warring had selected for her long ago. It was neatly parted on one side of her head, falling evenly to both shoulders. She was wearing makeup with light pink lipstick and matching nail polish. She looked every bit like a Princeton graduate, one who could easily have just stepped out of a Wall Street boardroom. As Jessie stood there smiling and waiting for the applause to die down, Molly's brow furrowed a bit. She was fixated on Jessie Warring's face, particularly her smile. There was something familiar. *No. It couldn't be. No way.*

When the applause died down, Jessie nodded and said, "Thank you all so much. It's such a pleasure to be here today. It feels like home, even though it's so far away from my beginnings back in Savannah, Georgia."

Maybe the reference to Savannah helped, but it was the unique, slight Southern twang in Jessie's voice more than anything that sparked Molly's memory. Without thinking, without realizing where she was, Molly leapt out of her seat and blurted out, "Blue! Is that you?"

There was a collective gasp from the audience as all heads turned toward the strawberry blond now standing in the second row. The men in black started to whisper into their microphones.

Jessie Warring froze, staring at Molly. Then her face exploded in joy as she yelled out, "Molly. Oh My God." She paused for a second, looked at the audience and said, 'Sorry, but you've got to excuse me for a minute."

Then Blue rushed from behind the podium and ran down the stairs fronting the stage as Molly pushed past the three people blocking her way to the aisle. The two men in black down on the floor quickly moved to cut off Molly's path. The dean of students, still on stage, watched in shock as the scene unfolded.

Blue reached Molly just ahead of the security guards, and she and Molly embraced, tears of joy flowing down their faces. Two seconds later, one of the men in black arrived and started to push Molly away. Blue gave him a dirty look and said, "Let go of her." He briefly backed off. In that split second of time, Blue leaned forward into Molly's ear and whispered, "I'll write you—in code. Please, I need your help."

And then the second guard arrived, preparing to break the young women up. Molly backed away from Blue under her own power. Blue gave the men another dirty look and walked back up the steps toward the podium as murmurs rippled through the audience.

When Blue got back to the mike, she took a deep breath, chuckled, and amped up her captivating Southern twang by saying, "I suppose y'all are wondering what that was all about, aren't you?"

A few in the audience let out a nervous laugh, but most stayed silent. Blue got a broad smile and said, "Sure you are!" And she was suddenly Jessie Warring again rather than Blue...back in control of the room as the audience broke into laughter.

Blue said, "Well, that wonderful young woman down there just happens to be the best friend I've ever had. We got separated when I went into foster care 10 years ago, and y'all just got to witness our spontaneous reunion."

Blue then looked directly at Molly and said, "In a lot of ways, we saved each other's lives back there on Tybee Island, didn't we Mols?"

Molly smiled, nodded, and held up her thumb for all to see as Blue concluded by saying, "But that's a story for another day, so now let me get to the reason I'm here."

For the next 45 minutes, Blue captivated the crowd with her pre-scripted, Warring-approved story. Molly, however, didn't hear much of it. Her mind was racing over the events that had just occurred. As happy as she was to see Blue, she couldn't make any sense out what she had just whispered into her ear.

A piece of the puzzle was solved when Blue wrapped up her presentation by saying, "In closing, I want to announce an exciting new initiative that we're kicking off at WWA. We all know that to be successful in the business world, it is imperative to have excellent communication skills. But what you may not appreciate is the incredible power of the written word. I don't mean quickly hammered-out text messages or tweets. I mean hand-written letters or notes. They create a personal touch that can bond for a lifetime. Ask yourself why you use the written word to send birthday cards, wedding wishes, and condolence letters to your closest friends and family. Why not a simple tweet or a text message? It's because we all intuitively understand that the hand-written word strengthens the meaning, the significance of our underlying message. This little tidbit of wisdom can be even more valuable in the business world. After all, it may help get you your next promotion, ink an important contract, or at the very least land you a bigger office."

She let the laughter subside and then continued, "But sadly, the young children of America are not being taught how to effectively communicate through the written word. In fact, many schools no longer even teach cursive writing. At WWA, we think this is a mistake, and to address this problem, I'm here to announce a new nationwide program at all our foster homes. We plan to double our efforts to work on every young girl's writing skills and help each of them to establish a pen pal to exchange letters once a week. To kick off this new program, I think it's appropriate that I ask Molly Nichols, my best friend, to become my pen pal. Mols, will you do that for me?"

Once again, Molly held up her thumb for all to see.

On stage, Blue smiled and said, "Terrific! Now if the rest of you follow suit, I think you will come to rediscover a certain joy, a bond that we've lost in this age of instant information exchange. Thank you all, and good afternoon."

As the students stood up and applauded, Molly left her seat and tried to move toward the foot of the stage. One of the men in black blocked her and motioned her toward an exit. Molly held her ground the best she could as she watched Blue tear off a page from her presentation and scribble something on the back. Then Blue waived off several admiring fans, including the dean of students, and quickly moved toward Molly. When she got to the edge of the stage, she knelt and held out the scrap of paper toward Molly. The security guard, standing between Blue and Molly, snatched it out of Blue's hand before Molly could take it. In that instant, Blue's demeanor changed, reminding Molly of a side of Blue's personality she had seen once before. Blue glared at the man and said, "Weren't you paying attention for the past five minutes? It's my mailing address for God's sake! You know, so we can kick off the pen pal program! Do you want to call my mother for permission?"

The guard quickly backed off, sheepishly handing Molly the paper. Blue stood up. Before returning to the other people waiting to talk to her, she looked at Molly and said, "Remember, this is important. Please don't let me down."

CHAPTER 6

MOLLY DIDN'T LIVE on campus. She was living with her dad, Jordan Nichols, in a nearby house he had rented. Jordan, in his mid-forties, had done a good job holding the signs of middle age at bay. His flat stomach was a by-product of a daily regimen of sit-ups and early morning five-mile runs. He still had a thick head of dark brown hair, although the grey had recently started to move in, and the only wrinkles on his face were the crow's feet that framed his light blue, deep-set eyes. With his well- proportioned, six-foot-tall frame, solid jaw line, and welcoming smile, he was a sought-after target of many single women, most of them on the rebound after a failed first marriage. But Jordan, while always gracious, didn't allow himself to get caught up in any romances. In fact, he didn't seem to enjoy life the same way he once had. He had never recovered from the murder of Molly's mother, his wife and soulmate— some 10 years earlier.

The reason for Jordan's recent move to Ithaca was to complete a long-postponed goal, a promise he had made to his dad to get a law degree. He was about to become the third son in a direct lineage, and the fourth man in his family with a law degree from Cornell. In fact, his father, Molly's grandfather, was Judge Jim, the man sitting on the New

York court charged with determining the constitutionality of the proposed New York LUV Act.

When Molly completed the 15-minute drive to the house, she found Jordan standing outside, waiting. As she pulled into the driveway, she gave him a big smile and a wave, anxious to tell him about her reunion with Blue. But by his body language, Molly knew something was wrong. She jumped out of the car and asked, "What's wrong, Dad?"

Jordan put his arm around Molly and, choking on his words, said, "It's your Pop. He passed away last night in his sleep."

Jordan started to cry. They embraced each other as Molly said, "But he seemed so healthy. What happened?"

"I don't know. Neither does Nana. I'm guessing it was his heart, but they're gonna do an autopsy tomorrow morning."

Jordan choked back some more tears and pulled away from Molly. "I'm sorry, Molly. I'm a real mess."

Molly, tears running down her cheeks, said, "That's okay. How's Nana doing? Shouldn't we check on her?"

"She seems okay. You know how stoic she is. But yeah, we do need to get over there. I already threw a few of my things in the car. Let's go inside so you can pack. I'm gonna stay with Mom for at least a couple of days, but you do whatever you need to with school and all. If you need to come back right away, you can drive back in my car, and I'll make other arrangements."

"I'm not worried about school, Dad," came the answer.

Jordan put his arm around Molly's shoulder, and they walked inside.

Twenty minutes later, they were on the road for the hour and a half drive to Oneida Lake. Something jolted Molly's consciousness, and she blurted out, "Oh! Aunt Jenna. Does she know yet?"

Jordan, keeping his eyes on the road, said, "Yeah. I tracked her down just before you got home. She and Uncle Rob are in Paris now. They're gonna make arrangements to get back as soon as possible, but I suspect it will take at least a couple of days."

"How was she? Did she seem okay?"

"Yeah. She's strong like mom—at least on the outside."

"I'll be glad when she gets here. I miss her so much."

"Yeah, me too."

They were quiet for about 10 minutes when Molly said, "You'll never guess who I ran into today!"

"Can you give me a hint?"

"Sure. She was my best friend from Tybee Island, the one we've both been searching for!"

"You finally found Blue?"

"Actually, it's more like she found me."

"Did you see her at that speaking event today?"

Molly smiled and said, "As it turns out, Blue *was* the speaking event. Dad, she's now Jessie Warring, the adopted daughter of Heather Warring!"

Jordan took his eyes off the road for a second, turned toward Molly, and said, "What?!"

Molly motioned for him to pay attention to his driving and said, "Yup. It was quite the reunion."

Jordan shook his head slowly from side to side and muttered, "Blue. I'm so glad you found her. Unbelievable. It sure brings back some bittersweet memories."

"Yeah, Dad. It does."

Molly watched her father wipe some new tears from his face and decided that telling him about what Blue had whispered into her ear that morning would have to wait.

CHAPTER 7

Dearest Mols,

Thank you so much for the very first official letter of the new pen pal program. With that said, I was so sorry to read about your Pop's passing. You and your dad have my deepest condolences. I wish I could somehow ease your pain, but it gives me comfort to know that you are staying with your dad for now. I know you will help each other through the healing process.

While this must surely feel a bit selfish given the circumstances, reading the rest of your letter truly lifted my spirits. It took me back to when we first met, and how much our friendship grew after that shaky start. (All thanks to me. Ha!) I know that I will never have a better friend than I have in you, even though it has been way too long since we last spoke.

Anyway, your letter also took me back to that wonderful trip we took with your dad to Disney World. That's my best memory of all. It was just the three of us in the happiest place in the world. Of all the parks, Magic Kingdom was my favorite. The Haunted Mansion, Big Thunder Mountain

Railroad, and the Pirates of the Caribbean still stick in my mind. Remember the end of the Pirates of the Caribbean ride when the boat goes under the bridge, and there's that cute little animatronic dog with the keys in his mouth? All the prisoners were reaching out of the cell, trying to get the dog to bring the keys over so they could escape. I guess they were really desperate.

Animal Kingdom was my second favorite park. Remember how embarrassed your dad was when we were waiting in line to see the 3-D movie inside the Tree of Life? I think the attraction was called "It's Tough to be a Bug" or "Stop Bugging Me", or something like that. Your dad's cell phone rang, and that cast membersmade him turn it off.

Tell you what! In your next letter, why don't you tell me what your favorite rides were. It will help make me feel like I'm a kid again. Anyway, gotta run now. Love you!

Jessie—aka Blue!

Molly, sprawled out on her dad's sofa, held out Blue's letter, and said, "Dad, take a look at this. It doesn't make any sense."

Jordan, pulling his eyes away from the evening news said, "You want me to read Blue's letter? In my day, pen pal letters were private."

"What do you mean *in your day?* I bet you never had a pen pal in your entire life."

Jordan smiled and said, "Okay, you got me. What's the problem?"

"The problem is that most of what Blue wrote about never happened. After offering her condolences for Pop's death, all she talks about is the time that we went to Disney World together. We never did that! In fact, I remember when you asked her to go with us. She refused. The entire letter, she's just making stuff up."

Jordan walked over to Molly, reached out, and said, "Okay. Let me see it."

Molly sat up, handed the letter to him, and walked out of the room toward the kitchen.

When she returned, soda in hand, Jordan looked up from the letter and asked, "Remind me, what exactly did Blue whisper in your ear that day?"

"She said something about writing to me in code. That she needed my help. But I can't find any code. I've tried reading it backward, every other word. You name it, and I've tried it."

Jordan winked at Molly and said, "Interesting. We'll have to call it Blue's Code!"

Molly shook her head and said, "Ha. Ha. And I bet you're just *dying* to figure it out."

Their conversation was interrupted by the sound of the doorbell. Jordan, glancing at his watch, asked, "Any idea who that could be?"

"Nope," came Molly's response.

Jordan walked over to the door and, without removing the security chain, peeked outside. He saw a face he recognized. It was that of William Bennings.

This can't be good.

He opened the door, and Benning's, a man

about Jordan's age, about five-foot, nine-inches tall with a small, athletic frame and short, black hair walked in. He was a man that always seemed on edge, the kind that brings a certain tension with them wherever they go. Bennings smiled and said, "Hi, Jordan. Good to see you after all these years."

Jordan nodded and said, "Really, Bennings. You sure it's good? Why are you here?"

"Ouch. What kind of greeting is that?" Then, Molly caught Bennings's eye, and he said, "And look at you! If it wasn't for the file photo, I'm not sure I'd even recognize you. Molly, you have really grown up"

Molly smiled, but Jordan glared at Bennings and asked, "What file photo? What the hell is this all about?"

Bennings held his hands out in front of him and said, "Whoa, sorry about that. Social skills are not my strong point. Let me start over."

Jordan said, "You do that! Start by telling us why you're here."

"Okay, but can I at least sit down?"

Jordan motioned toward a doorway and said, "In the kitchen."

The three of them moved into the kitchen and sat down at a small table tucked against the wall. Jordan walked over to the fridge, pulled out a Bud Light, turned, and asked Bennings, "You want one?"

"No, thanks."

Jordan sat down and asked, "What exactly is going on here?"

Bennings said, "Before I start, I need your word that this meeting and everything we talk about stays right here. Are you guys good with that?"

Father and daughter glanced at each other, and then Jordan said, "Yeah, sure. But first, let me see your creds. How do I know you're still with the Bureau?"

Bennings reached for his pocket as he smiled and said, "Always the cop." He pulled out a leather covered cardholder, flipped it open, and handed it to Jordan.

Jordan looked at the badge and the FBI identification card and handed it back as he said, "Okay, go ahead."

Bennings nodded and said, "A while back, I was put in charge of a team charged with investigating the deaths of seven individuals in various states across the country. What they had in common was that they all occurred in states where the LUV Act was being proposed and, with only one exception, all of the victims were key legislators arguing against passage."

Jordan immediately understood where the conversation was headed and said, "And that one exception was my father."

"You're getting ahead of me, but your instincts are right on point. The weird thing is that they were all ruled to be of natural causes."

Tears formed in Molly's eyes as she said, "Oh my God, Pop was murdered?"

Bennings nodded and said, "I believe so, but, unfortunately, we may never know for sure. Yesterday, my team was pulled off the case, and the case was closed."

Jordan asked, "Then why are you here?"

Bennings turned to Molly and asked, "Molly,

you're getting letters from Jessie Warring, or should I say Blue, aren't you?"

"Just one so far. But how did you know?"

"Not important, but would you mind if I take a look at it?"

Jordan didn't let Molly answer, interjecting a stern, "No." Jordan then looked at Molly and said, "Molly, please wait in the other room for a minute while Mr. Bennings and I have a word in private."

Molly said, "Yes, sir," and stood up and left.

Jordan moved uncomfortably close to Bennings's face and said, "Listen, Bennings, you've apparently gone rogue. I'm not going to put Molly in harm's way unless you start telling me what this is really all about."

"Fair enough. Do you remember last year's pandemic scare? The one that was predicted to be five times more deadly than Covid-19?"

"Of course. But they nipped it in the bud—came up with an effective vaccine before it even got out of China."

"And the company that came up with the vaccine?"

"Shit. That was Warring Pharmaceuticals. Wasn't it?"

"Yes, and they made a fortune on it with an exclusive government contract here in the U.S. and similar deals across the globe."

"So… how does this tie back to Blue?"

"Just give me a minute! What you need to know first is that, around the time of that scare, surveillance footage out of China turned up evidence of a meeting between a senior member of China's communist party and one of Warring's top executives. Based on that, we were authorized to wiretap Warring's external communications. Finally, two weeks ago, it paid off. We uncovered some text messages between Warring's senior security officer, Willard Lance, and a less than desirable character, the kind that deals in murder for hire. And guess what? We've been able to place him in close proximity to where at least four of the suspicious deaths occurred. Oh, and one of them was here in New York around the time your dad died."

"Did the director know all of this when he pulled the plug on your investigation?"

"You kidding? I think he pulled the plug *because* of it."

Jordan shook his head and said, "Seems crazy. Your boss was appointed by the incumbent President, and you'd think that the President, above anyone else, would want all the dirt he could get on Heather Warring."

"Yeah. You'd think so. But nothing in that town makes sense anymore. Just look at what happened to the last President. His own party turned on him simply because he was a political outsider. They fought him on health care reform, even fought him on closing the borders to illegals. Hell, they even fought him for trying to bring back jobs from China and make us energy independent. And then what happened? After that, we watched as local politicians forced the police to stand down while thugs in the streets were tearing down statues and looting stores."

"Okay, so maybe the country is turning to shit,

but you still haven't told me what that has to do with Blue's letter!"

"That day at Cornell, when Blue and Molly reunited, one of the few men I still trust was there in the auditorium. He's an old friend who helped me work the case back in Savannah. You know, when I first met you."

"Yeah, not good times."

"So, he knows all about Blue and Molly's past. When Blue invited Molly to be her pen pal, he took note that Warring's security team was anything but happy. He said Warring's top security officer, a guy by the name of Willard Lance, looked downright pissed off. And there was something else. He saw Blue whisper something into Molly's ear. So, I'm guessing that Blue knows what's going on at Warring Pharmaceuticals, and she's trying to pass that information along to us, through Molly."

"That is one hell of a leap of faith."

"Maybe. But at this point, it's literally all I've got. So, please, let me take a look at the letter. That's all I'm asking, and then I'll be on my way."

Jordan stood up and started pacing as Bennings watched and waited. Finally, Jordan stopped, looked at Bennngs, and said, "No. Not gonna happen. I am not going to put Molly in the middle of this. Now please leave."

Bennings head dropped, he took a deep breath, and then stood up.

"I understand, but please..." as he reached into his pocket and handed Jordan his card, "Call me if you change your mind."

Jordan escorted Bennings to the front door

where they said their goodbyes as Molly watched from her perch on the sofa. Bennings paused at the door, glanced over at Molly, and said, "Nice to see you again, Molly. You take care now."

Jordan closed the door behind him.

Alone with Molly, Jordan walked over to her and asked, "What are you doing tomorrow morning?"

"Nothing. Why?"

"How about we both get a good night's sleep, and tomorrow morning, we take a closer look at Blue's letter?"

CHAPTER 8

JORDAN SAT AT his kitchen table reading Blue's letter as Molly watched and waited. When he finished, he put the letter down and looked up at Molly who said, "See, Dad, it doesn't make any sense."

"Maybe, but let's try looking at this from a different perspective. She told you that she was gonna use some sort of code. Other than the two of us, who would know that the Disney trip never took place?"

"No one, I guess."

"So, don't you think that just maybe, Blue's code is hidden in...."

Molly eyes lit up as she interrupted, "Of course. It's in the stuff she made up! Why didn't I think of that?"

"Well, I am the detective in the family."

Molly smiled and said, "Okay, detective, then let's get started. As I told you, I've already tried reading it backward, reading every other word, every third word, just the first letter of every word. You name it, and I've tried it."

Jordan nodded and said, "What if it's simpler than that?"

"How? In what way?"

"I don't know yet." Jordan pointed toward the kitchen counter and said, "Go grab a pen and a piece of paper from the counter."

Molly walked to get the pen and paper as Jordan continued, "I'll read the part of Blue's letter where she's talking about the Disney trip, and you jot down any key words or sayings that jump out at you."

With Molly taking notes, Jordan read.

Anyway, your letter also took me back to that wonderful trip we took with your dad to Disney World. That's my best memory of all. It was just the three of us in the happiest place in the world. Of all the parks, Magic Kingdom was my favorite. The Haunted Mansion, Big Thunder Mountain Railroad, and the Pirates of the Caribbean still stick in my mind. Remember the end of the Pirates of the Caribbean ride when the boat goes under the bridge and there's that cute little animatronic dog with the keys in his mouth? All the prisoners were all reaching out of the cell, trying to get the dog to come over with the keys so they could escape. I guess they were really desperate.

And Animal Kingdom was my second favorite. Remember how embarrassed your dad was when we were waiting in line to see that 3-D movie inside the Tree of Life? I think the attraction was called "It's Tough to be a Bug" or "Stop Bugging Me", or something like that. Your dad's cell phone rang, and that cast member made him turn it off.

Tell you what! In your next letter, why

don't you tell me what your favorite rides were. It will help make me feel like I'm a kid again. Anyway, gotta run now. Love you!

    Jessie—aka Blue!

When he finished, Jordan looked at Molly and asked, "What did you write down?"

Molly said, "Not much. You were reading too fast."

"That was intentional. Just read me your notes."

"Okay. I've got "haunted mansion, big thunder railroad, pirates of the Caribbean."

Jordan interrupted and said, "Stop. Skip the names of the rides. Just focus on Blue's descriptions of them."

Molly looked at her notes again and said, "Okay, she only describes two of them, Pirates of the Caribbean and the Tree of Life. Let's see, for the Pirates of the Caribbean, she used words like *bridge, dog, keys, prisoner, escape, desperate*. Wait! Now I see where you are going with this!"

"Good. So, what is it telling you?"

"She's desperate—a prisoner. She's trying to escape? Those security guards were all over her at Cornell. But, still. She's 25 years old. How could she possibly be a prisoner?"

Jordan said, "Hold that thought. What did she say about the Tree of Life?"

"Let's see. That was in Animal Kingdom. Words like, *it's tough to be a bug, stop bugging me, cell phone, cast member, turn it off.* Does that mean that Blue's cell phone is bugged?"

Jordan smiled and said, "That would certainly explain why she has to write to you in code. She doesn't trust using her phone, and she's probably afraid they are also reading her letters. I think she is, in effect, a prisoner—a damn smart one at that!"

Jordan studied the letter again and, without taking his eyes off of it said, "It looks to me that whenever she's trying to pass along information in code, she starts the sentence with the word *remember.* And she's also telling you how to communicate back to her. She's asking you to tell her what your favorite rides were. She's set up a framework so you two can go back and forth in code without anyone picking up on it. Blue, I am impressed!"

"So, now what?"

He looked at Molly and said, "I honestly don't know." Then Jordan pulled out his wallet and fished out Bennings's card. As he looked it over, he said, "Tell you what. You work on a letter to send back to her. Try using her code so she knows you've figured it out, and ask how we can help. In the meantime, I'll call Bennings. I guess it can't hurt."

"Okay. Thanks, Dad. I love you."

"Love you too, pumpkin." He winked at her and smiled.

Molly smiled back, shaking her head from side to side. Every once in a while, Jordan still loved to call her *pumpkin,* her childhood nickname, knowing how much it embarrassed her. Deep down though, Molly still loved it—just not when anyone else was in the room.

CHAPTER 9

PEANUT WAS LYING on her bed watching TV in her new room. It was the smallest of the four bedrooms in the private living area of the governor's mansion, and it sat just inside the hallway door that lead to the rear foyer. She heard a familiar knock and Blue's voice from the other side of the door, "Hey, Peanut, it's me. Can I come in?"

Peanut sat up and said, "Yes! I've been waiting for you!"

Blue opened the door, came in, quietly closed the door behind her, and locked it.

Blue said, "Sorry I couldn't go with you today. How'd it go?"

"Pretty good. Travis took me all the way to Atlanta, to a specialist at the Winship Cancer Institute at Emory University. They have me scheduled for some tests in a couple of days."

"Good. I'll go with you. Isn't it amazing how quick they can see you when you're staying at the governor's mansion?"

"Yeah, guess so."

Blue suddenly put her finger up to her mouth, whispered "hush," and motioned for Peanut to follow her. Blue walked to the closet door, got down on her knees, and disappeared under some of Peanut's clothes that were hanging on the lower of two rods that spanned the width of the closet.

When Peanut got to the closet, all she saw was her clothes, but she heard Blue whisper from behind them say, "I'm back here, just crawl underneath."

Peanut followed Blue's instructions and found herself in an open space running the full width of the closet for six feet to a rear wood paneled wall. Peanut grinned childishly and said, "This is really neat. Does anyone else know it's here?"

Blue, speaking very softly said, "They have to. Heck, when there's no clothes hung in the closet, you can see all of this."

Peanut, disappointed with the answer, said, "Yeah, guess you're right."

Blue smiled and said, "But nobody else knows about this!" She stood up and walked all the way to the back wall of the closet. Then, she put both hands on the top left side of the paneled wall and gave a quick, hard tug to the right. The wall moved, sliding almost all the way into the plaster wall beside it. Beyond the new opening in the wall was nothing but darkness.

Peanut's eyes lit up. She looked at Blue and asked, "A secret passageway?"

Blue smiled and said, "Yup. Before my mother moved in, she had an elevator installed, the one out in the foyer, the one I'm not allowed to use. When they did that, they sealed off a doorway out there that led to a stairway down to the lower level. Supposedly, back when Governor Joe Brown lived here in the 1850s, the servants used that stairway to bring food and drinks up to the governor and his guests. But when they put in the elevator and covered up that door, they didn't know that there was a second, secret way to get to the back stairs and...ta da! This is it."

"How did you find it?"

"When I was a kid, I had my own little hideaway in a cubby-hole in my room. My dad built it for me. When my mom got sick, I'd go in there to be alone."

"That's so sad."

"Yeah… so when we moved here, I took this room because the closet reminded me of my old cubby-hole. And then one day, I was sitting back here in the corner and leaned against the wall. I heard the paint crack, and then a rattle in the door, and that's how I found it. My guess is that it was put here so that Governor Brown could sneak his favorite slave girl up here for you know what after his wife fell asleep down the hall."

"You mean, they did it right here, in my bedroom?"

"Yup. Either that or it was set up for a servant to help with a baby or something."

Peanut smiled and said, "I like that explanation a lot better."

"Well anyway, tomorrow, I'll show you some more. Are you up for an adventure?"

"I guess so. Where are we going?"

"Down the steps that are behind the door. When we do, we need to be really quiet, because if we get caught, we're screwed."

"Then why are we doing it?"

"Because I love a good adventure. Don't you?"

"I guess so."

"Good. We'll do it together, early tomorrow night."

CHAPTER 10

THE SUN WAS setting as dust filled the air behind the silver, 2010 Ram 1500 truck pulling an open trailer full of landscaping equipment down a Georgia dirt road. Behind the wheel was Taylor Riggs, a 34-year-old, six-foot-two African American. He had a shaved head, brown eyes, and high cheekbones. His sweaty T-shirt had been thrown onto the passenger's seat, revealing a physique that looked to be straight out of a print ad for the latest home fitness gimmick. His upper left arm, currently resting on the truck's window ledge, sported a tattoo of an American Flag waving in the breeze with the words *Semper Fi* directly underneath.

Riggs turned off the road onto the gravel driveway of a modest mid-60s era red-brick ranch house. The house was more than 200 yards away from its closest neighbor and had three acres of farmland directly behind it that was full of fall corn. Riggs pulled to a stop and rolled up the truck's window, quietly cursing the truck's broken air conditioner, as well as the unusually hot October day he had just endured. He grabbed his T-shirt from the passenger's seat, used it to wipe sweat dripping from his forehead and brow, and jumped out of the cab.

As he turned toward the house, he heard several cars approaching. He turned back to see two black

BMW 750s with tinted out windows fly by, kicking up dust behind them.

Slumming it. Must have been an accident out on 441.

Riggs cupped his hands to his mouth and called out, "What's the matter, Gov? Gotta mingle with us common folk today?" And then he turned toward the house as the door opened and a four-year-old boy ran out yelling "Daddy!"

Holly, the boy's mother and Riggs's wife, appeared in the doorway to watch as Riggs kneeled down, said, "Devon, my man," and scooped up the little boy into his arms.

When Riggs got inside, he set Devon down and watched Holly carry a serving plate of steaming-hot roasted turkey into the room and set it down on the dining room table. Holly said, "Here ya go, honey. Just in time. It's fresh out of the oven."

Holly was pure country girl, including the heavy Southern twang that politicians and late-night talk show hosts like to make fun of. She was on the thin side, with round cheeks, light brown skin, brown eyes, and a smile that made everyone who saw it feel like it was meant just for them. After the turkey was all but gone and Holly had settled Devon into bed for the night, she looked at Riggs and asked, "Do you really have to go to that meeting tonight?"

Riggs nodded and said, "I'm sorry, honey, but I do. We're losing our country, and we can't just stand by and let it happen."

"But I heard the guys talking down at Kroger's today, and they we're saying some things that scare me. They're good guys and all, but you are the only Brother in the bunch. If they do some of the things they're talking about, you know who they're gonna blame."

"You know better than that. These are my friends, and this is our home. No one's gonna come after me. Besides, I'm the one trying to keep them out of trouble. I can't let Eddie and the others go off the tracks. I'm all for protesting, but we've gotta do it the right way. And I won't be late. Frank's gonna be here early tomorrow with the harvester."

"Oh, that's right. Heck, he'll have our three little acres of corn done in an hour."

Riggs laughed and said, "I'll bet it's less than that. Gives him more time to sit down and eat some bacon and grits Remember, you've gotta feed him when he's done!"

Holly laughed and asked, "How could I possibly forget?"

Then Riggs saw the headlights through the windows and heard the horn. He smiled at Holly and said, "Sorry. Gotta run. Eddie's here."

"Okay, hon. Just don't be late. Love you."

Riggs walked to the door, looked back, and said, "Love you, too." He disappeared into the night.

CHAPTER 11

BENNINGS, SITTING AT Jordan's kitchen table, handed Jordan Blue's letter and said, "So, if Blue's being held prisoner and her phone's been tapped, Warring must be afraid that she might spill the beans about something!"

Jordan laughed and asked, "Spill the beans? Haven't heard that one since I was a kid. Anyway, Molly's already got a letter drafted that uses Blue's code to ask her what we can do to help. Anything you'd like to add?"

Bennings stared off into space for a moment and then turned to Jordan and said, "Yeah, there is. See if Molly can figure out a way to let Blue know that I'm heading down there, to Milledgeville. I want to snoop around a bit, especially out at Warring Pharmaceuticals. I think it's about 50 or 60 miles out of town."

"How are you gonna pull that off with the case officially closed?"

"How? That's simple, I'm gonna retire."

"Retire? What are you, like 45 years old?"

"Give or take. But, like I already told you, something big is going down, and I think Warring is right in the middle of it. All I see, or should I say smell, in D.C. anymore is a giant sewer, and I figure I have a better chance of fixing it as a private citizen than working for the turds running the shit show."

Jordan stood up and started pacing. When he sat back down, he looked at Bennings and said, "Well, I've put off my law degree for over 20 years so far. I don't think another six months is gonna matter."

"What? You going with me?"

"Might as well. Maybe we can see if the devil really did go down to Georgia."

Bennings smiled and held out his hand.

Jordan shook it and said, "Oh, and by the way, I'd suggest you get out and buy some jeans and T-shirts."

Bennings nodded and said, "I know. And maybe some *camo*. Too!"

CHAPTER 12

BLUE REACHED THE bottom of the steps, turned around, and told Peanut, "You can relax now. Nobody's down here." She turned off the flashlight on her iPhone, and Peanut got her first glimpse of the eerie world that existed within the two-foot-wide space between the temporary walls of the war room and the original plaster walls of the governor's mansion.

Thin streams of light, seemingly cut by a laser into large square patterns, flowed in from the war room through gaps around the television monitors. As Peanut's eyes adjusted, she saw large bundles of electrical cables that ran along the floor with offshoots spidering up to the television monitors as the cable made its way around the perimeter. She saw aluminum supports that ran from the top of the temporary walls and angled over her head to the base of the original walls.

The two-foot-wide path surrounding the entire war room could be navigated, but it required both caution and patience.

Blue motioned for Peanut to follow her. They slowly worked their way around the perimeter, ducking under support beams and weaving their way around cables. When they reached a large brick-lined fireplace, Blue pointed to it. They stepped inside the hearth, giving them more room. Blue had to kneel, but Peanut was short enough to stand. Blue smiled and asked, "Sorta cool down here, isn't it?"

Peanut, looking around at the fireplace said, "Yeah, I wonder if they cooked right here, in this fireplace?"

"Good question."

"What would happen if your mom ever found out we were here?"

"Don't know. Don't wanna know! But as long as were careful, the only way that will happen is if a worker comes back here to fix something and sees us."

"How do they get in?"

"There's a door built into the war room. I used it to sneak out there once, just to see what was there. Want to check it out?"

"No, thanks!"

Their conversation was suddenly interrupted by the sound of the bookcases opening. Blue put her finger to her lips and motioned for Peanut to stay where she was while Blue ducked out from the fireplace and peeked through the opening next to one of the monitors. She saw her mother standing by the conference table, talking to Brandon Newsome, Warring Pharmaceutical's senior vice president of sales and community relations. Blue had only met him once or twice, but she recognized him immediately by his perfectly groomed silver hair. He looked exactly the way he was supposed to, as a man who spent most of his adult life wining and dining the bureaucrats and politicians of Washington D.C. in return for favors directed at Warring Pharmaceuticals. Blue put her ear against the wall just in time to hear her mother ask, "More trials? I thought we were past that!"

"So did Dr. Shulman. But several patients have started to revert. Last night, we lost contain on one of them, a 20 year old, and she couldn't be saved."

"That's impossible. Shulman supposedly mastered the sequencing code months ago. What the hell is going on out there?"

"Please, I'm only the messenger. Shulman started mumbling about Yamanaka factors, misaligned pluripotency, and on and on. I don't have a clue what any of that means. All I know is that I was called in to help with the bio cremation. Why me, I'm not sure."

"Stop complaining. We all have to do our share."

"I understand, but really?"

Warring ignored the comment and asked, "How much more time does he need?"

"He said he'd have a new sequence ready for trial in a couple of weeks. Then it'll be at least a couple of months until we know if it works."

"Damn him! This could not be worse timing. Look, keep this strictly between us. Make sure that Shulman and his team keep their mouths shut."

"Yes, ma'am. Oh, and one other thing."

"Just what might that be?"

"We need a few more trial participants."

"Talk to Lance and have him harvest them out of WWA. He knows the procedure. Now, if you don't mind, I have an important phone call to make."

Newsome nodded and walked past the sensor. After the doorway opened up, he left the room.

Warring walked over to the conference table, took a deep breath, and dialed a phone number. By chance, the monitor that Blue was standing closest to suddenly flashed on, startling her. She regained her composure in time to see her mother look in her direction and say, "Mr. President, I'm told that you wanted to talk to me."

From the voice box at the conference table, Blue heard the unmistakable voice of Mark Reynolds, the current President of the United States say, "Yes. I wanted to tell you that I have decided to accept your offer. I'm ready to join."

"Congratulations. You won't regret your decision."

"Thank you. Does this make me a card-carrying member of the Deep State, or is there something more that you require from me?"

"Mr. President, we don't refer to ourselves by that name. We are the Guild, and yes, you are now a card-carrying member. But you already know the rules. You can never tell anyone that you are a member of the Guild, nor can you disclose our name. If that would happen for any reason, you will be immediately terminated. Sorry to put it so bluntly, but I was told the exact same thing when I was asked to join, and it applies to all members equally, even to those on the governing counsel."

"And who comprises the governing counsel?"

"I can guess many of the names, but no one knows for sure. Maybe someday soon, we will all know."

"But how do you communicate—even operate—under those restrictions?"

"On the principal that communication only occurs when it is essential to the completion of a specific task, and then, it is restricted to only those assigned to that task. Long ago, the governing counsel established a framework, using what they refer to as *progress pods*. Each pod is established for a very specific purpose or task, and only members deemed essential to achieve that purpose or task are put into that pod. For example, I was notified, along with several others, that I was being assigned to a progress pod for the specific task of recruiting, and subsequently mentoring you in the ways of the Guild. It is only when you are working within an assigned pod that you may come to know other members. Otherwise, we all remain anonymous. It seems odd at first, until you come to realize that it helps protect all of us individually while also serving the Guild's long-term objective. What I've found very beneficial about it is that, when I am not assigned to a pod, I can continue to live my life in exactly the same way as I always have. And when I am assigned to a pod, I am always given all of resources required to achieve it, which includes access to, and the required use of, state-of-the-art encryption and electronic communication tools."

"Okay, I get it. We're a modern-day Knights Templar, Freemasons, or Skull and Bones."

"With one significant difference. We are using today's technology to leverage power, wealth, and wisdom in order to..."

The President interrupted and said, "I know... in order to make the world a better place! Speaking of that, how is your own work coming along? After all, you used that little tidbit of information to recruit me."

"You are correct, I did. But that was at the direct instruction of the governing counsel. But now that you are one of us, I can only repeat what you already know, that the End Game will be initiated during my first term as President. There will be some suffering, some bloodshed, and a massive redistribution of wealth. But it will be well worth it in the end."

"Thank God that's all gonna go down on your watch!"

"Sir, you are being far too myopic. You need to work on that."

"I guess you're right. I do feel very privileged."

"As you should. Our world is about to change forever, and you are now going to be on the right end of that change. But now, I have to run, so welcome aboard."

"Thank you and good day, Governor—or should I say Madam President?"

Warring laughed and said, "No, that can wait. One thing at a time."

With that, she hung up the phone and the screen went dead.

Blue, listening from the other side of the wall, stayed frozen in place until Heather Warring left the room. Then she turned around to face Peanut and said, "Wow! Maybe I shouldn't have heard that. Could you hear it from back there?"

Peanut nodded, closed her eyes, and asked, "Can we get out of here?"

Blue quietly said, "Yes. It's time to go."

CHAPTER 13

IT WAS LUNCHTIME at Bully's Bar and Grill, and Jordan was one of about a dozen patrons sitting in the main dining room. Set in the heart of downtown Milledgeville, Bully's was the kind of place that every Southern town has—a place where the drinks are cheap and the food tastes good, even if it's not good for you. Bully's menu was pure Southern, and most everything other than the burgers saw the bottom of a deep fryer, even the pickles. The owner and head cook was an overweight, bald-headed, 45-year-old man known by everyone as Ducky. With his deep booming voice and quick smile, Ducky was easy to like.

Bully's décor tended toward rural farmer, if there is such a thing. Old sickles, rusty hay hooks, and other miscellaneous farm tools decorated the walls. Inside the front door, a cornucopia full of fake fruit spilled out onto a red-and-white-checkered tablecloth covering a hay bale that sat directly behind the cash register. A Formica counter fronted with a stainless-steel strip of metal stretched the entire length of the main dining room. In the morning, the locals sat there to eat their grits, pancakes, and bacon. As the day wore on, the same people came back in after work for a cold beer or a shot of whiskey.

Across from the counter was a row of booths, each with their own window and view of the parking lot. At the far end of the booths, there was a separate room that could seat 15 for private gatherings. Based on the yelling coming from behind the door, Jordan could tell the room was currently in use.

Jordan, sitting in the booth closest to the main entrance, finished his fried chicken, wiped his fingers using a paper towel ripped from the roll sitting in front of him, and turned his attention to his iPhone. He scrolled through a couple of photos until he found what he was looking for: a picture that Molly had sent him of the latest letter from Blue.

Dear Molly,

Hope this letter finds you well. I know we've pretty much exhausted recounting our Disney experience, but I wanted you to remember the very last ride we went on— the Tower of Terror. Remember how freaked out I was after we entered the mansion and Rod Serling said we were about to step through a door and into a nightmare? From then on, everything on that ride was almost unbelievable—impossible to explain. In fact, I'm getting scared now just thinking about it.

But let's talk about something new. I want you to bring me up to date on how your art is coming along. I hope you are still painting because you're the best. One of my favorites has always been that sad painting of the young girl standing outside of the cancer clinic with a tear in her eye. Even though you would never admit it, I still think you painted that for me because of what happened to my mom. You captured the fear and loneliness that young girl must have been feeling at the time. In fact, right now I have a young friend, I call her Peanut, who's facing those same fears and loneliness. She's fighting lymphoma, but thanks to my mom, I'm able to be there for her.

Mom let Peanut move in with us here in Milledgeville and has gotten her the help she needs at Winship Cancer Institute at Emory University, in Atlanta. Speaking of Atlanta, I need to cut this letter short to give me time to prepare for my upcoming quarterly WWA board meeting at the Georgian Terrace. Cool hotel!

Anyway, in your next letter, please tell me about your favorite paintings and what makes them special to you. Are you still doing some of those seascapes that you loved to paint?

Love,

Jessie—aka Blue!

Jordan set down his phone and glanced outside just in time to see Bennings hop out of a white Toyota and head for the door. The two of them had flown into Atlanta the day before, rented the car, and driven the 100 miles to Milledgeville. When they got there, they had checked into Star's Bed and Breakfast, an old Southern, Victorian-style home about four blocks from Bully's. Bennings was now returning from a field trip some 60 odd miles out of town where he had checked out Warring Pharmaceuticals, while Jordan had used the time to scout Milledgeville on foot.

As Bennings approached Jordan's table, Jordan asked, "So, did you see what you wanted to see out there?"

"Pretty much. But the place looks more like a prison than a campus complex for a private pharmaceutical company."

Jordan nodded, held out his phone, and said, "Here's the latest from Blue."

Bennings took the phone and sat down across from Jordan, but he was quickly distracted by the shouting going on in the back room. He looked up and asked, "What the hell is going on back there?"

Jordan shrugged and said, "Good question. They're definitely pissed off about something."

"Do you know who is in there?"

"No, but based on all the trucks outside, I'm guessing it's a bunch of good ol' boys."

"Yeah. This lifestyle is gonna take some getting used to." Glancing at the remnants of Jordan's fried chicken, he added, "Including the food."

Jordan laughed and said, "Yeah. I'm gonna need to do some extra sit-ups, that's for sure."

Bennings refocused on Jordan's phone and said, "Let's see what Blue has to say."

As Bennings studied Blue's letter, an attractive waitress in her early forties approached their booth.

She had a small frame, shoulder-length brown hair pulled back in a ponytail, light green eyes, and freckles. She was wearing Bully's official uniform: a white apron over black slacks and a black-and-white checkered blouse. Flashing a mouth full of white teeth, she looked at Jordan and, in a pleasing Southern accent said, "I see your friend's finally here."

Bennings, focusing on Blue's letter, didn't look up.

Jordan shook his head, winked at the waitress, and said, "Earth to Bennings, earth to Bennings. Do you copy?"

As Bennings pulled his eyes away from the phone Jordan said, "Ah. There he is. Bennings, this is our waitress, Kylie. She's a sweetheart, so please, take your nice pills."

Bennings said, "Hi, Kylie, pleased to meet you. But don't let him fool you, I'm the good guy on this team."

Kylie laughed and said, "I'm sure you are. Now, can I get you anything, or would you like to see a menu first?"

"Uh, for now just a cup of coffee, please. No cream, no sugar."

As Bennings refocused on the phone, Jordan looked at Kylie and added, "If you don't mind, would you bring me a Bud Light?"

Kylie smiled and said, "Sure, sweetie, be back in a minute." She flashed another smile at Jordan before turning away with a purposeful flip of her ponytail. This time, Bennings noticed. He put the phone down, smiled, and said, "Am I missing something, or is she flirting with you?"

Jordan blushed a little and said, "No way. She's just looking for a good tip. And everyone calls you sweetie down here, so get used to it. Now what do you think of the letter?"

"To me, it looks like Blue's Code has just been upgraded to Release Number Two. She wants to use Molly's paintings, imagined or real, as a second way to communicate. Makes total sense. It will give both of them more flexibility. As for the Tower of Terror, I think she's seeing or hearing things that are freaking her out. Notice how she referred to the ride as being inside a mansion? The Tower of Terror is in an old hotel, not a mansion. Clever!"

"I agree. Oh, and the reference to a painting of a girl with cancer has to be a bogey of some sort. I know all of Molly's paintings, and that's not one of them."

Bennings nodded. Reaching out, he said, "Let me see your phone again."

After scanning the letter a second time, he handed the phone back to Jordan and said, "Molly's last letter let Blue know that we'd be down here, right?"

"Yeah. She worked in a reference to the small world theme ride."

"Good. Because I think Blue's trying to give us two different options on how we might be able to meet up with her. This Peanut girl must be for real, and she must have cancer. Otherwise, whoever's reviewing her letters would know she's lying, and that would put them on notice. So, she's telling us that one option is to meet with her in Atlanta at the Cancer Treatment Center."

Jordan nodded and said, "Yeah, but we don't know when, or how often they go there. Won't be easy."

"Agreed. In the meantime, it should be on the public record as to when the next WWA board meeting is. But if we go there, we're gonna need Molly's help. You okay with that?"

"Why? What are you thinking?"

"We'll need her to try and isolate Blue away from her security. Maybe Molly shows up to surprise her best friend and then pulls her aside."

Jordan said, "Yeah, but we'll still need a way to get Blue completely alone...maybe the ladies' room or something. If Blue's telling it like it is, they will be all over her."

"I know. We can figure the rest out later, but right now, I'm hungry. You drink your beer, and I'll order something. It will give you another chance to talk to Kylie, or is it sweetie?"

****

Twenty minutes later, Jordan and Bennings were standing in Bully's parking lot when the door swung open and about a dozen men, ranging from their late twenties to mid-forties walked out. They were wearing work clothes and talked amongst themselves until they saw Bennings and Jordan. Then their conversation ground to a halt. As they moved past, some of them gave a cold stare, while others just looked at the ground.

Jordan turned to Bennings and quietly asked, "Doesn't look like we're very welcome here, does it?"

"You think?"

Seconds later, Bully's door swung open again. A skinny, pockmarked, 30-year-old white man wearing a red bandanna around his forehead, jeans, and a sleeveless Harley shirt staggered out, holding a can of beer. He stumbled down the steps and fell right into Bennings's arms, beer splashing onto his shirt. Bennings grabbed the man by the shoulders, stood him up, and asked, "Hey there, buddy, don't you think it's a little early for that?"

The man pulled his eyes into focus and said, "I'm not your buddy, buddy! Mind your own damn business!"

Bennings was a man with a short fuse. He grabbed a fistful of the man's Harley shirt and was about to shove him up against the car when he heard a deep voice behind him say, "Hey! Go easy on him, or you'll have me to answer to."

Bennings turned and saw Taylor Riggs, all 240 pounds of him, standing at Bully's front door in faded jeans, a white T-shirt, and a straw, sweat-stained cowboy hat.

Jordan glanced at Bennings and then quickly turned to Riggs and said, "Sorry, mister. We didn't start this. Just trying to cool this guy down. Is he with you?"

Bennings eased up on the man as Riggs said, "Yeah. He works for me, and he's also a good friend. Just let him go, and we'll be outta your way." Riggs turned to the man and said, "Eddie, go wait in my truck, okay?"

Eddie pleaded, "Come on, we can take these guys. They're government stooges. I can smell it."

Riggs gave Eddie a stern look and said, "I said... go wait in the truck!"

Eddie gathered himself up, shook his head, and begrudgingly walked toward Riggs's truck. Riggs looked at Bennings and said, "Sorry about that. Eddie's been on edge lately, and right now, he's a little drunk to boot."

Jordan said, "Yeah, I can see that."

Bennings quickly eyed the tat on Riggs's arm and said, "Former Marine, I see."

Riggs frowned and said, "Nope. No such thing!"

Bennings nodded and said, "Oh yeah, that's right. Once a Marine, always a Marine." And then he extended his hand for a handshake and said, "William Bennings, former Ranger, third battalion. You can call me Bennings, like everyone else does." Pointing to Jordan, Bennings added, "This here is Jordan Nichols, former police detective."

Riggs nodded and said, "Taylor Riggs," as he shook their hands. "What brings you two to Milledgeville? Did Eddie get it right?"

Bennings glanced at Jordan and said, "Hell, no. We're here for the duck hunting. Heard it's good out this way, so we came in to check it out and maybe hire a guide. You do that sorta thing?"

Riggs, not convinced, shook his head from side to side and said, "Nope."

Jordan glanced toward Riggs's truck and said, "Mind if I ask what's bothering your friend Eddie over there? He doesn't seem to like government folk all that much."

"Let's just say that none of us country boys are all that pleased with what's going on these days.

Unless you've been living under a rock, you know they're trying to take away our guns, and that isn't gonna fly down here in Georgia—no more than those make-believe ducks you came here to hunt."

Bennings smiled and said, "Yeah, I guess not."

Riggs nodded and said, "Well, nice meeting you." and then turned and walked to his truck, leaving Bennings and Jordan behind.

CHAPTER 14

BENNINGS LOOKED AT himself in the full-length mirror one last time. Then, he turned to Jordan, who was doubled over laughing, and said, "If you take one picture, or tell a soul, I swear on my mother's grave that I will kill you."

They were in a room at the Georgian Terrace, a historic grand hotel in downtown Atlanta that sits directly across the street from the Fox Theatre on Peachtree Street NE. Bennings was dressed in full drag, including a woman's gray pantsuit, a brunette wig, and makeup.

Jordan temporarily composed himself and said, "Well, at least you're not wearing a dress!" and then burst out laughing again.

Bennings couldn't help but laugh along with him. Out in the hallway, someone put a room card into the reader slot, and Jordan quickly walked to the door and asked, "Who is it?"

The door swung open, and Molly walked in saying, "Who else? This is my room, you know."

Jordan said, "Anyone following you?"

"No. We're good. Blue's not even here yet."

Molly looked at Bennings, waggled her head, and said with a smile, "My, my, aren't we the pretty one?"

Bennings said, "Okay, enough! Your dad's been

on me all morning. We need to go over the plan. The WWA board meeting is at 1:30 in a room off the lower lobby, one floor below the main lobby, right?"

Molly said, "Yes. It's posted up in the main lobby and says that the area will be closed to the public between 1:00 p.m. and 3:30 p.m. I went down and checked it out. There's a ladies' room right near the conference room where the meeting is being held."

Bennings said, "Good. I'll head down to the ladies' room and set up shop inside one of the stalls. As soon as you see Blue, you do the *surprise* thing, hug her, and then get her to go into the ladies' room. And remember, Blue doesn't know we are here, so you may need to be creative. Make sense?"

Molly nodded and said, "Yup. With any luck, her security team won't let anyone else in so you and Blue should be alone in there."

Jordan said, "In case security does a sweep ahead of time, when you get in there, lock the stall door and keep your damn feet up."

Breaking into laughter again, he added, "Maybe you can do a little spidey-man act, using the stall's walls."

Molly joined in with laughter as Bennings stood there, shaking his head, a big grin on his face.

****

When Travis pulled Blue's limo to the curb on the left side driveway of the Georgian Terrace, Willard Lance's two-man security detail was already in position. One of them stood at the lower-level side entrance to the hotel and watched as Travis emerged from the driver's seat and quickly moved around to the rear curbside door and opened it for Blue. The second man was positioned inside, in the main lobby, which was one floor up.

The hotel, a prime evening gathering spot for big events around town, was relatively quiet early in the day. As Blue and her security escort moved inside to the small foyer, Travis jumped back into the limo to park it in the nearby parking garage.

Inside, the only two options presented to most visitors were to either walk up an open, marble staircase or to take an elevator up to the main level. VIP's using the lower level boardrooms, however, were given an additional option. Next to the elevator, a hotel staff member waited for Blue, holding open a door to a back hallway that provided Blue and her security guard direct access to the lower lobby where the board meeting was being held. It eliminated the security risk of having to parade dignitaries up to the main lobby, only to have them walk back down a wide-open center staircase to the conference rooms.

Long before Blue arrived, Bennings had taken up his position in the ladies' restroom. Molly, assuming that Blue would be walking through the main lobby, had settled into one of the many leather chairs up there and waited. She watched as the board members arrived, checked in with the security guard at the top of the steps, and then walked down the staircase. After more than 45 minutes had passed, Molly saw the guard looking down the stairway and talking into his lapel microphone. Her instincts told her something was wrong. She stood up and casually moved toward the staircase, hoping for a better view.

Molly's suspicions were confirmed when she heard Blue's voice echoing up the marble stairway. Molly glanced down and saw Blue at the base of the stairway chatting up several board members. Molly and Blue's eyes briefly met as Molly's mind raced to develop a backup plan. A second later, she got a pained look on her face, put her hands on her stomach, rushed up to the security guard, and loudly announced, "Can I please use the bathroom downstairs? I have a real problem."

"Sorry, ma'am, but you'll have to find another one. I'm sure there's another one up here somewhere."

Molly then screamed at the guard, "Sir, if you won't let me use that bathroom down there, you will be responsible for any accidents."

As Molly turned and stormed off, a knowing smile crossed Blue's face.

For the next few minutes, Blue continued to talk to her fellow board members. Then she said, "Now, if you'll please excuse me, I need to make a quick trip to the ladies' room. Why don't the rest of you head into the board room. I'll be right there."

As Blue turned toward the ladies' room, the guard standing by her held up his hand and said, "Please, Miss Warring. Let me do a quick sweep. It'll only take a second."

Travis, who had just arrived through the back hallway, heard the guard, and more importantly, read the look on Blue's face. He looked over and said, "No worries, Jeff, I got this."

He changed direction, knocked on the ladies' room door, asked, "Anyone in here?" and walked in. Seconds later, he reappeared, held the door open, and said, "Go ahead, Miss Warring. We're all clear."

As Blue walked past Travis, he gave her the slightest of nods. As soon as Blue was safely inside the ladies' room, she whispered, "Anybody in here? This is Blue."

Bennings emerged from the stall, pulled off his wig, and with his finger to his lips, whispered, "I'm Detective Bennings. Remember me?"

Blue suppressed a laugh and in hushed tones said, "I do, I think. Thanks for coming."

Bennings said, "Look, we don't have much time, so tell me everything you know and what we can do to help."

She nodded and said, "My mother's up to something really scary inside the plant. I heard her talking to one of her employees about patients who are out there, how one of them died, that they bio-cremated her, and that they are harvesting trial participants from WWA. There's a doctor. His name is Shulman, I think. He works out there, and he's doing something with sequencing codes and Yamanaka factors. Oh, and two minutes later, my mom got a call from the President, and he said he wanted to join the Deep State."

"Woah! Do you mean POTUS? The President of the United States!"

"Yes!"

"Okay. Circle back for a second. What about these Yamanaka factors?"

"I looked it up, and they have something to do

with stem cells and something called pluripotency. I'm pretty sure it has to do with regenerating body parts. You can look it up."

Bennings said, "Roger that. Now, what about the President and the Deep State?"

"The President said he was joining her team and asked if he was now a card-carrying member of the Deep State. She said yes, but it wasn't called that. It was called something else, uh, I'll think of it. And then they talked about a governing counsel, and how they... Wait! It's the Guild; that's what they call themselves. And they communicate using something called progress pods. Then she talked about initiating an End Game during her first term as President. It's gonna include bloodshed, redistribution of wealth, stuff like that."

"Holy shit! This is even crazier than I thought!"

There was a loud knock on the door. From the other side, the guard asked, "Miss Warring, you all right in there?"

Blue calmly but sternly said, "Of course! I'll be right out."

Bennings waited a few seconds and whispered, "Okay, we've only got a few minutes, but we still need to talk some more. Is this Peanut girl for real, and if so, can we meet when she goes for treatments?"

"Yes, and yes. She's living with us at the mansion, and she's going to the Winship Cancer Institute at Emory for treatments. Our driver, Travis, the guy who just came in here to check out the bathroom, I think he'll be driving when Peanut goes to the hospital. You can trust him."

"What day and time?"

"This Wednesday at 10 a.m. I'll be with her, unless my mother says otherwise."

"Good. See you then. If you need us, Mr. Nichols and I are staying at Star's Bed and Breakfast on Warren Street. Now go, get out of here."

Blue waited until Bennings moved out of sight from the door, glanced in the mirror, fixed her hair, and walked out. As Blue moved toward the meeting room, she looked at Travis and said, "Travis, I think I forgot my lipstick. Could you please check for me?" Then she turned to the security guard and said, "I'd like you to join me in the board room if you don't mind. I need some help with the projector. Travis can handle it out here."

A minute later, the ladies' room door opened, Travis stuck his head in, and said, "Whoever you are, now's your chance."

Bennings appeared from inside the stall and asked, "How'd you know anyone was in here?"

"A look from Jessie. Now get out of here and take the door to your left. It leads to the back hallway."

Bennings paused at the bathroom door and said, "Thanks, I take it that you're Travis."

"At your service."

Bennings smiled, nodded, and quickly exited the bathroom. As Travis watched, Bennings opened the door to the back hallway and disappeared.

CHAPTER 15

ON WEDNESDAY AFTERNOON, Peanut, Blue, and Travis were sitting in the waiting room at the Winship Cancer Institute. It was a large room, with dozens of patients and loved ones spread out, waiting for their names to be called. When the nurse came out to take Peanut back for her radiology treatment, Blue stood up, gave Peanut a hug, and said, "Good luck. I'll be waiting right here when you're done."

When the wooden door closed behind Peanut, Travis stood up and asked, "Mind if I leave you alone for a few minutes?"

"Not at all. Where are you going?"

"I'm hungry. I need some real food."

"You mean the kind you can wash down with a beer or two?"

"Guilty as charged. But, I promise, no more than two beers. After all, I gotta drive you guys home."

"Travis. Please, make it just one!"

"Deal. Call me as soon as she comes out. I'll pull up curbside within five minutes of hearing from you."

Blue nodded and said, "I'll see you soon."

No sooner had Travis left than a man sitting nearby, reading a newspaper, put it down and walked toward Blue. He looked down at her and asked, "Blue, do you remember me?"

Blue broke into a broad smile, jumped up, and held out her arms for a hug. She asked, "Mr. Nichols, how could I ever forget you?"

Jordan hugged Blue, pulled back to take her in from head to toe and said, "You have grown up to be such a beautiful, successful young woman. I couldn't be any prouder of you."

Blue's smile weakened and she said, "Yeah, well, things aren't always what they seem. Are they?"

"I understand. Bennings told me everything, and that's why we're here."

Jordan turned away from Blue and motioned Bennings over, who had kept his distance during Jordan and Blue's reunion.

Blue looked at Bennings, smiled, and said, "Awww, and you were such a beautiful woman."

Jordan laughed and said, "Well, at least you still have your sense of humor."

Bennings smiled and said, "Okay enough of that. Can we find a more private place to talk for a couple of minutes?"

Blue said, "Yeah. Peanut won't be out for at least a half-hour. We can walk outside."

When they reached the sidewalk by the parking lot, Blue said, "I'm so glad you came. I need to get away from my mom as soon as possible. Peanut, too. I'm really scared."

Jordan said, "We understand. But unfortunately, we could use your help from inside the mansion. We need some names, some planned activities by this so-called Guild that we can act on. Can you help us?"

"I think so. But I can only hear things by sneaking

into my mother's war room. I don't scare easy, but well, you already know what I've been hearing."

"If I can get you some listening devices, do you think you could hide them down there somewhere?" Bennings asked.

"I don't think it would do any good. She had some super high-tech jamming equipment put down there that won't let any unauthorized signals get in or out. I heard her talking to a security contractor before we moved in. Besides the jamming equipment, every signal that gets in or out of that room, even on the TV screens, gets encrypted somehow."

Bennings nodded and said, "Well, maybe something as simple as a digital recording device behind the walls could work, even an iPhone. Let me talk to a specialist I know who still works for the Bureau, and I'll get back to you. In the meantime, hang in there. We'll try to figure out a way to get you out. It's not gonna be easy."

"I know. She's watching me more than ever."

"Understood. As for now, what can you tell us about the layout of Warring Pharmaceuticals? Have you ever been inside?" Bennings asked.

"Yes. I've been there three or four times, usually so Mom could show me off to someone making a big contribution to WWA or some high-end pharmaceutical client."

"What we're most interested in is their security setup and where their research is being done."

"Well, I know they have cameras everywhere. They monitor them from a room just inside the main entrance to the building. When you go in, there's a security checkpoint where you wave your access badge on a scanner. Behind the counter, there's a security guard who processes visitors, and behind that guard, there's a room where all the monitors are."

"Any idea how many people they have monitoring the cameras?" Bennings asked.

"One, maybe two at most. It's a pretty small room."

"Any chance that you have your own access badge?"

"I do. In fact, I keep it in my purse."

"Could we borrow it?"

Blue reached into her purse, pulled the badge out, and pressed it into Bennings's hand. "Take it. If anything goes wrong, I'll just say that someone stole it."

"Thanks. Now what about the research area? Is there any part of the complex that seems extra secure, maybe off limits to almost everyone?" Bennings asked.

"Yes! I was never allowed on the second floor. In fact, I never even saw a stairway. Anyway, I need to get back inside now."

Blue gave Jordan a quick hug. As she did, Jordan slipped a piece of paper in her hand and said, "That's my cell phone number. Memorize it, and then throw it away. I know that your phone may be bugged, but if you ever need help, we can be there in a heartbeat. Take care. I owe you my life."

Blue smiled and said, "No, you don't." Then she turned and walked back inside.

Twenty yards away, a silver Chevy Traverse pulled out of a parking spot and headed toward

Bennings and Jordan. The driver, a pasty-faced man in his mid-fifties with round, wire-rimmed glasses and slicked-back blond hair, slowed his car and stared at Bennings and Jordan as he drove past. Bennings looked at Jordan and said, "Wow. Nothing subtle about that."

"Nope. We better let Blue know that we've been spotted."

The driver was Willard Lance, Warring's head of security.

CHAPTER 16

IT WAS 8:30 a.m., and Heather Warring had just dismissed her team from one of their twice-a-week campaign strategy sessions. As they filed out of the war room, Willard Lance remained behind. When the bookcase closed, Lance opened a manila file folder, slid it in front of Warring, and said, "Here are the photos. I had them printed so they'd be easier to review."

Warring opened the folder, pulled out a stack of glossy pictures, and quickly flipped through them. Then she closed it, looked at Lance, and asked, "Who are they?"

"The shorter one is William Bennings, former FBI. Get this: He was the man heading the task team charged with looking into our operations related to both the Covid vaccine and the LUV Act."

"You mean the one that I had closed down?"

"Yes."

"And who's the man with him?"

"Jordan Nichols, the father of Jessie's long-lost friend, the one she met up with at Cornell."

"You mean her pen pal friend?"

"You got it."

"Well, Mr. Lance, it would seem that we have a problem, so what is it that you suggest we do?"

"I'm not sure yet. If we come at these guys

head-on, we're likely to attract more attention than we need right now. Whatever we decide, it needs to be well thought out."

Warring stared off thinking for a moment and then turned to Lance and said, "Willard, I think I have a different way to approach this."

She pushed some buttons on the panel in front of her, and Jimmy Harris, her campaign manager, soon appeared on the monitor.

"Good morning, Governor," Harris said. "Sorry I couldn't attend the meeting, but I've been busy working on the logistics of the upcoming convention and the hit list of friends and family we're trotting out to sing your praises."

"A bit early for that, isn't it?"

"Never too early. But what is it that I can do for you today?"

"Are you alone?"

"Of course. I take all your calls in complete privacy. In fact, I have to. The encryption technology is here in my private office."

"Good, because I was just wondering: If a hypothetical female candidate running for high political office had something tragic happen to one of her children, would that have a positive or a negative impact on her candidacy?"

Harris smiled through his tobacco-stained teeth and said, "A grieving mother running for office? Unless the death was due to parental negligence, a drug overdose, or something quite scandalous, the election would turn into a blow-out. She'd have the vote of every mother in America, guaranteed."

"Thank you, Jimmy. That's all I needed to know. Good day."

Warring hung up the phone, and Harris's face disappeared from the screen.

Warring looked at Lance and said, "And that's how you turn a problem into an opportunity. To be clear, it needs to happen soon, and it needs to be tragic in nature. Perhaps a car crash—hit by a drunk driver in broad daylight. Oh, and Peanut might just as well be in the car with her. Do you have any problems with that?"

"No, ma'am, of course not. But before I go, I need you to see one other thing." Lance quickly scanned through the pictures until he found what he was looking for. He handed the picture to Warring, pointed to something, and said, "See that? Right there. Jessie's got something in her hand, and she's giving it to Bennings. Trouble is, I can't make out what it is."

Warring nodded and said, "Well, that's just one more reason to eliminate the problem. Two weeks from tomorrow, I'm scheduled to appear at a rally in Boston with Jessie on stage with me. Perhaps my personal tragedy should occur shortly after that while poor Jessie's image is still clear in everyone's mind. Understood?"

"Yes, ma'am."

"Good. We're done here . In the meantime, please continue to monitor all of Jessie's communications. We must remain diligent, Mr. Lance. Always diligent."

"Yes. Of course."

CHAPTER 17

BENNINGS WAS SITTING in the passenger's seat of the Camry. Jordan was driving. They had just pulled off a rural road 60 miles northeast of Milledgeville, and Bennings was looking at Warring Pharmaceuticals through a pair of binoculars. Unlike most of the other big pharm companies, Warring Pharmaceuticals had only one location where all research, manufacturing, marketing, and management originated for the family-run empire. The complex sat on more than 100 acres of wide-open land surrounded by a security fence, complete with razor wire at the top, that formed a tight perimeter around the buildings and the parking lot. The fence sat about 50 yards back from the road. To get beyond the fence, you had to check in with a security guard at an outside gate.

"You were right," Jordan said. "It does look more like a maximum-security prison than a pharmaceutical company."

Bennings pulled down his binoculars and said, "Yup. This is the third time I've been out here, and I've learned a little more each time."

"Like what?"

"Little things. Who comes and goes. When the shifts change. And today's Sunday, so I wanted to see what kind of shift, if any, they were running today."

"Look any different than during the week?"

"Actually, it does. Look at the parking lot. It's only 10 percent full. The other two times, it was packed."

"Yeah, but I bet the staffing of the security team stays the same."

"Probably. But let's move down the road and turn around, just out of sight of the guardhouse. I want to sit awhile and see what kind of commercial traffic they have going in and out of here on a Sunday."

"You think that's our ticket inside? Hitching a ride on a delivery truck?"

Bennings nodded and said, "Maybe. We do have Blue's entrance badge, but I'd rather not dress up and try to..."

Jordan cut him off laughing and said, "What! Dress up like Blue, or should I say Jessie Warring and then just sashay right on in there?"

"Actually, yes. I think I could pull it off. You know I did work undercover for the FBI for over 10 years, and I happen to know the best makeup man in the business!"

Jordan laughed and said, "Yeah, right. You'd end up looking more like Mrs. Doubtfire than Jessie Warring!"

Bennings smiled and said, "Well, we'll never know because I think we have better odds if both of us hitch a ride in on a delivery truck. From there, I'm hoping that we can use Blue's card to open doors if we need to."

"Well, they sure as hell are gonna have cameras, and likely some big dudes standing around the loading dock to onload and offload stuff."

"Unless you have a better idea, just shut up, settle in, and we'll see who comes and goes."

Twenty minutes later, Jordan broke the silence and asked, "What would you think about adding some sort of a diversion?"

Bennings turned to him and asked, "What are you suggesting?"

"Remember that Marine we met at Bully's?"

"Yeah, his name is Riggs. So what?"

"Well, he and his buddies certainly don't have a warm spot for Heather Warring or any politicians. We might be able to talk them into holding a protest rally outside of Warring Pharmaceuticals on the day we're breaking in."

"Yeah. I like it. Wait! What's this?"

Bennings pointed to a mid-size lift-gate truck with its left turn signal already on as it passed their car. The signage on the side read *Bell's Bakery, Food, and Catering Service, Milledgeville, Ga.* Forty yards further down the road, it turned left into the entrance of Warring Pharmaceuticals. Bennings picked up his binoculars, and in a command and control voice Jordan had never heard before said, "Don't pull out until I say otherwise, and then move slowly up the road, emphasis on slowly!"

Jordan, sarcastically responded, "Roger that, sir!"

Bennings smiled but kept his binoculars on the back end of the truck as the driver waited at the gate for the guard to let it pass. When Bennings saw the truck start to move forward, he said, "Okay. Pull out and drive slowly, so I can see where that truck heads. Please!"

As Jordan drove past the plant, Bennings continued to peer through his binoculars. He saw the truck move through the parking lot, go along side of the building, and then disappear around the back. He lowered the binoculars and said, "Perfect. Loading dock is in back, out of sight. Now all we have to do is check out this bakery's base of operations. How lucky can we be? They're somewhere in Milledgeville! Now, on to your idea. I got Riggs number off the side of his truck the other day. I'll give him a call and see if we can buy him lunch."

CHAPTER 18

JORDAN AND BENNINGS were sitting at Bully's talking to Kylie when Riggs walked in the door and approached their booth. When Riggs saw Kylie, he paused and said, "Hi, Kylie. How are you doing these days?"

Kylie smiled and said, "Good as can be expected. How's that little one of yours? Bet he's growing like a weed."

"Sure is. Stop by some time. I know Holly would love to see you."

"I'll do that."

"Great! You take care now, ya hear?"

"Will do."

The exchange didn't escape Bennings. As Kylie walked into the kitchen and Riggs sat down next to Jordan, the first words out of Bennings mouth were, "I couldn't help but notice that you're friends with the waitress. What's the story with her anyway?

Jordan looked at Bennings and said, "What the hell?" at the same time that Riggs asked, "In what way?"

"Well, I don't see a ring on her finger, and I'm pretty sure that Jordan here has a bit of a crush on her!" Bennings continued.

Jordan stared at Bennings and said, "You never

quit, do you? and then turned to Riggs and said, "I'd like to apologize on behalf of Bennings here. I know you're a busy man."

Riggs smiled and said, "No, that's okay. I couldn't blame anyone for eying her up. She's about as nice as they get. She lost her husband a little over a year ago to a drunk driver. Damn shame. She's got a 15-year-old girl at home. But that's not why you called me here, so let's get to it."

Bennings nodded and said, "Okay then. Here's the deal. The three of us have more in common than you might think, and we need your help."

"How so?"

"We need you and as many of your gun-loving friends as possible to stage a pro-gun, pro-Second-Amendment protest rally out at Warring Pharmaceuticals. Nothing where anyone gets hurt, just a noisy, sign-toting mob denouncing Heather Warring as an enemy of the Second Amendment."

"What are you up to? Almost sounds like some sort of a diversionary tactic."

Bennings said, "You saw action. Didn't you? I can tell that you think like a Marine—one who's seen some combat."

"Yeah. Operation Iraqi Freedom. I was all of 18 years old."

"That was Regimental Combat Team 1, right?"

"You know your history. But you're avoiding my question."

"Look, the less you know right now, the better off you are."

Riggs said, "In that case, the answer is no. I

don't even know who you guys really are, and I don't know what kind of trouble I might be putting my friends in the middle of."

Riggs started to stand up when Bennings grabbed hold of his forearm and said, "Just look me in the eye, bro, and I promise, you'll know what I'm all about. I love this country every bit as much as you do, and right now, we need your help. I just walked away from the FBI because of the things I've been seeing and hearing in Washington. Truth is, I think we're fighting for more than just the right to bear arms."

Riggs pulled away from Bennings's grip, but he slowly sat back down. He looked at Jordan and asked, "What about you? Where do you fit into all of this?"

Jordan exhaled and said, "Fair question, one that I keep asking myself. Right now, all I can tell you is that I know someone who, not by choice, is in very close proximity to the governor, and that individual has reenforced everything Bennings just said. Trouble is, right now we have no proof. That's what we're working on, and it's why we need your help."

Riggs didn't answer right away. He sat there in thought, rubbing his hand over his shaved head as Bennings and Jordan exchanged worried glances.

Finally, Bennings broke the silence when he said, "Look at it this way, Riggs. If you and your friends make the evening news for a peaceful protest, that's a good thing, right? You're protesting for what you believe in. In the meantime, it will be us two taking all the risk. Come on, what do you say?"

Riggs stood up, looked down at both of them, and said, "Give me a week's notice, and I can get about 50 of my friends out there, making as much commotion as you'd like."

Bennings looked up at Riggs towering over him, smiled, and said, "Thanks, Riggs, and Semper Fi!"

****

That same night, at 9:30 p.m., Jordan walked into Bully's alone. Kylie was still there, busy wiping the counter down when she looked up and saw him. He smiled and pointed to his regular booth. She smiled back and nodded, so he walked over and sat down. A minute later, Kylie came over, sat down across from him, and said, "Jordan, you know we stop serving at 9. Don't you?"

"I do. But I didn't stop in to eat. I wanted to talk to you for a couple of minutes," Jordan smiled and added, "Without my nosy partner along."

Kylie returned the smile and said, "Oh. Okay. What would you like to talk about?"

"I'd like to tell you a few things about myself."

Kylie nervously glanced around and said, "Well, I only have a few minutes, but go ahead. I'm listening."

"First off. I just heard about your loss, and I'm very sorry."

Kylie choked up a bit, looked at Jordan, and said, "Thank you. I won't say it hasn't been difficult, but between my family, the good Lord, and a few friends...my daughter and I...well, we manage. Some days are better than others, if you know what I mean."

"I do. At least I think I do. Ten years ago, I lost

my wife. She was murdered. Since then, my daughter and I, well we've seen our share of struggles as well."

Kylie reached out, patted Jordan's hand, and said, "Oh, I'm so sorry."

"That's okay. I just wanted to be up front with you because, well, you're the first woman, since... in the past 10 years that I've felt any kind of connection to. I like you. That's all I came in here to tell you."

Kylie smiled and said, "That's so sweet. I'm really flattered."

"Really?"

"Yes. Really."

"Well, then maybe, sometime down the road, do you think we could meet for lunch or dinner?"

She smiled and said, "Only on the condition that we do it out of town. This place is way too small, and the folks are way too nosy for you and me to be seen out and about."

Jordan smiled and said, "Deal!"

Kylie said, "Good."

Jordan stood up and said, "I better get out of here so you can clean up."

As Kylie stood up, Jordan paused on his way out the door and said, "Don't tell Bennings, okay?"

Kylie smiled and said, "Wouldn't think of it!"

Jordan walked out into the night air.

CHAPTER 19

BENNINGS AND JORDAN were little more than shadows against the wall as they moved down the hallway and toward the steps of Star's Bed and Breakfast. The creaking floorboards of the 100-year-old house were their only concern in terms of drawing the attention of another guest.

Jordan followed on Bennings's heels as they went down the steps and slipped out the front door and into the night. Once outside, they didn't talk. They kept a fast pace through the side streets of Milledgeville for seven blocks until pausing in front of an old, one-story brick building with the Bell's Bakery, Food, and Catering Service logo painted on it. It was only 5 a.m., but the sweet smell of fresh bread already filled the air.

Bennings motioned his partner to follow as he moved along the side of the building toward the back. When Bennings turned the corner, he saw what he'd seen on his surveillance run: a row of four delivery trucks facing out from their bays on a loading dock. Bennings, cutting between the trucks and the loading dock, soon found truck number 2884. It was a box truck with a roll-up rear door. Bennings pointed to the latch and gave Jordan a quick thumbs up. It wasn't locked.

Here goes.

Clang! Bennings pulled on the latch and slowly lifted the truck's door just high enough to squeeze underneath. Jordan went first. He laid flat on the truck bed and slid under the opening. Then Bennings slid the backpack they brought with them underneath the door and followed suit.

As soon as Bennings cleared the door, he stepped on the inside handle, closing the door. Bennings stood up, grabbed his backpack, and scanned the truck. Wide shelves ran down each side, designed to hold food bins that could be locked into place. The cab was open, allowing the driver to access the rear of the truck through a center walkway between the driver's and passenger's seats.

"What do we do about the latch?" Jordan asked. "We left it open."

Bennings nodded and said, "Wait here. I'll take care of it."

Bennings walked toward the front of the truck, through the walkway to the cab, and slid into the driver's seat. Then he checked out the door locks.

Good. Old school. He pulled up the driver's side door lock, opened the door, and went around back to re-latch the roll-up door. When he returned, he found Jordan curled up between the back of the passenger's seat and the shelves. Bennings sat down across from him, behind the driver's seat, and said, "Okay. All systems go."

"Now what? Did you know this was an open cab? We're sitting ducks in here."

Bennings smiled and said, 'There you go with that duck thing again." He opened his backpack and pulled out two small black tarps. He tossed one at Jordan and said, "That's why I brought these. Put it over your head and settle in. At six in the morning, no one is very observant—especially after a late Saturday night."

"I'm not so sure."

"Just do it, and stop complaining."

"Yeah, whatever."

Thirty minutes later, Jordan was startled by the sound of a ramp being pulled out of a slot under the truck and getting slammed into place between the loading dock and the truck. A minute later, the trucks roll-up door latch clanged open, and a strong yank sent the door clattering its way to the top of the truck.

Bennings and Jordan stayed motionless under their tarps as a young man rolled a stainless-steel food transport cart into the truck and down the center aisle. The man removed sealed food containers from the cart and latched them into place on the shelves. He repeated the process three more times, each time moving closer to the back of the truck. Finally, Bennings and Jordan heard the driver's side door get yanked down and the ramp being shoved back into the slot underneath the truck bed.

A few minutes later, someone yelled, "We ready to roll?"

Another voice replied, "Yup. She's all loaded for you, Benny. See you tomorrow."

The door of the cab opened. A man jumped into the driver's seat, started the truck, and pulled out of the lot.

****

An hour later, the truck was within 15 miles of Warring Pharmaceuticals. The driver, a middle-aged man with thinning black hair, was singing along with an old Dean Martin song when Jordan slipped out from under the tarp, pulled out his 9mm Glock from a side holster, and used it to softly tap him on his shoulder.

The driver said, "What the!?" His eyes popped when he saw the gun pointed at him and he said, "Mary, mother of Jesus!"

"Just stay calm, mister," Jordan said. "We're not gonna hurt you. We just need your help."

"We? What's going on here?"

Bennings popped up from behind the driver's seat. Looking at the driver in the rearview mirror, he said, "It's Benny, right?"

"Yeah. How'd you know?"

"Look, Benny. Just follow instructions, and you won't get hurt, you'll get your truck back, and we'll all live happily ever after."

"Hey. Just take the damn truck. I won't even look at you. Please, I got a wife and kid at home."

Jordan pointed out the passenger's side window to a wide shoulder on the road ahead and said, "There. Just pull the truck off the road up there, and we'll explain what we need you to do."

Benny glanced back at Jordan who still had his gun trained on him said, "You're gonna kill me; aren't you?"

Jordan pulled down his Glock and said, "Will you relax! No, we are not gonna kill you. You have our word. We just need your help to get us into Warring Pharmaceuticals. After that, you'll be free to go. Truck and all."

As Benny pulled the truck off the side of the

road, he asked, "So, you guys wanna break in there?"

Jordan said, "Yeah."

"Well, if it helps, I don't like the lady that owns it. She's trying to take our guns away, and us Italians don't like that anymore than the rednecks."

Jordan laughed and said, "Yeah, I know. I got some Italian in me as well. You don't have a gun in here. Do you?"

"No. No way. We're not allowed."

"Good. Now here's what we need you to do..."

****

Twenty minutes later, when Warring Pharmaceuticals came into sight, Benny asked, "What the hell is goin' on up there?"

Bennings, peeking over the seat smiled and said, "How about that! They really came through!"

They were looking at a group of about 40 protestors, marching around in front of Warring Pharmaceuticals' fence, pumped signs in the air that read, "Warring stomps on the Second Amendment," "If at First You Don't Secede, Try Try Again," and "You Will Never Take Our Guns." As the food truck got closer, they heard the protestors chanting "Warring's gotta go!" over and over. When the truck pulled into the entranceway, the protestors quickly blocked it. From behind the driver's seat, Bennings said into a walkie-talkie, "Good job, Riggs. Let us past now, and in five minutes, go to phase two."

"Roger that" crackled back through the walkie-talkie.

The crowd parted, allowing the truck to pull up to the guardhouse by the gate. Jordan ducked back behind the passenger's seat while Bennings took the risk of peeking out the front window again. *Local press is here. Perfect!*

After the truck was cleared, Benny passed through the gate, proceeded around the building, and backed into the loading dock. Before Benny could hop out, Jordan whispered, "The keys, Benny?"

"What! You don't trust me?"

"Well, I did just hold a gun to your head."

Benny handed Jordan the keys as he said, "You got a point."

Bennings said, "Like we told you, you drop us off in the kitchen on your first run, and then, after you're done with all your deliveries, just wait for us there. Got it?"

"Yeah, I got it."

Five minutes later, Benny rolled the food transport cart, covered by a tarp, through an empty hallway and into the kitchen. He stopped and said, "Okay. It's all clear. Now get out! You guys weigh a freakin' ton."

Nichols rolled out from under the tarp and onto the floor with Bennings right behind. Jordan stood up and said, "For Christ's sake, Bennings, you didn't have to shove your feet into my face."

"You wanna know where yours were?" Bennings asked.

Benny chuckled and said, "You sure you two know what you're doing?"

"No. But thanks for the help anyway." Bennings replied.

"Yeah, whatever. For what it's worth, the hallways are still empty, but the kitchen help gets here in about 45 minutes, so don't be late."

Benny took the food cart and left as Bennings and Jordan scanned the room. They found themselves on the service side of a cafeteria, standing where Benny would soon be sliding his sandwiches, fruit cups, and desserts into angled stainless steel bins so that employees on the other side could move their food trays along rails and pick out what they wanted.

Jordan looked at Bennings and asked, "You really think we can trust him?"

"Nothing we can do about it now. Let's split up and try to find a way to the second floor. If you find something, call me on the walkie-talkie. Otherwise, let's meet back here in five minutes."

Jordan nodded and said, "I hope phase two works."

"Roger that. And remember, no guns. If we get caught, we surrender."

"How the hell did I ever let you talk me into this?"

Outside, phase two went into effect. Under Riggs's direction, Eddie pulled a life-size effigy of Heather Warring out of the back of his trunk, tied it to a stake, poured gasoline on it, and set it on fire as the news cameras rolled.

Inside the complex, the chief of security was on the phone listening to instructions from Heather Warring as she screamed, "I don't give a damn. You get your entire team out there, and shut down that camera crew. Then you do whatever else needs to be done to end this thing. Bust heads if that's what it takes. Now go!"

As five guards scrambled outside to get the protest under control, Bennings and Nichols moved quickly through the halls, searching for a stairway or an elevator to the second floor. Five minutes later, they met up outside the cafeteria.

Jordan asked, "No luck?"

"Nope."

Jordan said, "Son of a bitch. This is a complete…"

Ding! A chime rang out from around the corner. The men exchanged glances and took off running toward the sound. As they rounded the corner, they saw what appeared to be a five-foot section of solid wall slowly swinging out at a 90-degree angle.

Seconds later, a thin, 70-year-old man with wiry white hair, wearing a lab coat walked out from behind the wall. He was lost in thought and staring down at notes on a clipboard, so he didn't see Bennings or Jordan at first. When he was no more than 10 feet away, Bennings stepped in front of Jordan and announced, "Good morning. You're Dr. Shulman; aren't you? Governor Warring sent us out here to meet with you."

Shulman stopped in his tracks, looked up from his clipboard, and asked, "Oh? And who are you?"

Bennings said, "My name is Dr. Russell, and this here is Daryl, my assistant. We were asked by Miss Warring to check on your progress. She's very upset about the recent setback."

Shulman started to fidget, took a step back, and said, "No one told me that you were coming. Can I see some credentials please?"

Jordan, impatiently watching, reached behind his back, pulled out his Glock and asked, "Will this do? Now, if you don't mind, just take us to the second floor." Shooting a look at Bennings, he added, "By the way, my name is not Daryl."

Shulman said, "Uh. Well, okay, since you put it that way. You're not gonna get away with this. We have guards everywhere."

"They're busy right now, so move it," Jordan said.

Shulman nervously walked toward the wall, which had closed, moved up to an eye scanner that was mounted on it, and the wall reopened. When it did, it revealed an elevator.

The elevator door opened, and all three of them got in. Bennings scanned the hall as the door closed. With the elevator moving up, Shulman said, "You know this won't do either of you any good. There's another security system up where we're headed that even I can't circumvent."

"We'll take our chances," Bennings said. "Just cooperate, and you'll be unharmed."

When the elevator doors opened, Bennings and Jordan found themselves walking into a spotless, sterile room of white walls, white cabinets with stainless steel countertops, white ceilings, and white floors. The only natural light filtered in from a long row of windows placed high along the outside wall to the rear of the building. Temperature monitors everywhere all read precisely 70 degrees. Dozens of high-tech microscopes and specialized machines sat on the stainless-steel countertops. Some were circular in shape, some looked like microwaves. On the wall opposite the windows, seven doors were spaced out across the room.

"I told you; there's nothing here!" Shulman said.

Nichols pointed to one of the machines sitting on a counter and asked, "What's that thing?"

"That thing, as you call it, is a centrifugal concentrator."

"What's it used for?"

"To remove unwanted solvents, so we can concentrate—or isolate—certain cells."

Bennings and Jordan exchanged looks, with Jordan saying, "Okay." Pointing to another piece of lab equipment, he asked, "What about that thing?"

"That is a hybridization incubator. It's used to maintain precise temperature and humidity control over the samples we test."

Jordan smiled wryly, glanced at Bennings, and said, "Okay, now we're getting somewhere. What type of samples are you testing?"

"You wouldn't understand."

Jordan pulled out his Glock, waved it at Shulman, and said, "Try me."

"The work we are doing here is beyond your ability to understand. It has to do with stem cells, regeneration, and the ability to cure all diseases by reversing the sequence in which they occurred. Now if you'll please put the gun down and go home, maybe someday you will be able to benefit from our research."

"I rather doubt it," Jordan said as he tucked his gun back into his pants.

Bennings wasn't paying attention to any of this. He had walked over to one of the doors, opened it, and disappeared inside. He found himself in a dark room, about 12 feet deep. At the far end was a large, circular fish tank about 6 feet tall and 8 feet across. Inside, was a school of tiny jellyfish, emanating vibrant color from within their bodies as their long tentacles danced in the water.

Bennings poked his head out from the closet and asked, "Hey, Doc, what's this all about?"

Shulman whipped around and ran toward Bennings as he said, "Let them alone. They're a hobby of mine. I've always loved jellyfish."

"Is that so?" Bennings asked. "The label on the tank says *Turritopsis dohrnii*. Unlike my partner here, I happen to know a little something about science."

"Hey, Daryl," Bennings said, turning to Jordan. "Wanna guess what these little guys are famous for?"

"My name's not Daryl, and no, I do not want to guess."

"They're immortal jellyfish," Bennings said. "They have the ability to reverse their own aging process. They can pretty much live forever."

Bennings's tone changed, and he looked Shulman in the eye and asked, "You're trying to play God here, aren't you, doc? Screwing with the meaning of *life ever after!*"

Schulman didn't answer. He was focused on Jordan, who was walking toward another door, just to the right of the first one. Jordan swung the door open and said, "Behind door number two, we have... Oh boy! They're also playing around with the meaning of *till death do us part.* I might not know anything about immortal jellyfish, but I sure as hell know what an alkaline hydrolysis machine looks like. And I know what it's used for as well."

Bennings walked over and looked at what Jordan was talking about. "What the hell? Looks like a souped-up tanning bed."

"Yeah. I call them pressure cookers. You put a dead body in there, and an hour later all you have left is a few ashes and a little bit of goo. Everything else has been melted down the drain, using a combination of chemicals and pressure. It's the new *green* way to dispose of a human body."

Turning to Shulman, Jordan said, "Get over there. Stand by the pressure cooker and smile. I want a picture."

Shulman said, "I will not."

Bennings grabbed Schulman by the arm, pushing him into the room as he said, "Yes, you will."

Jordan took a picture with his iPhone as Bennings moved toward the remaining doors and asked, "Anything else hiding behind these?"

Bennings quickly moved from left to right, opening the remaining doors. All were unlocked and all held nothing more than storage closets for medical gowns and miscellaneous equipment—until he got to the last door. It was locked, and unlike the others, it was made of solid steel. Bennings turned to Schulman and said, "Open it."

Shulman said, "I can't."

Bennings said, "You can't, or you won't?"

Bennings and Jordan exchanged glances. Bennings nodded, and Jordan pulled out his gun and said, "Stand back."

He took aim at the lock when Shulman yelled,

"No! You might hurt someone. Here, I'll open it for you."

Shulman fidgeted around in his pocket until he found a key card. He walked up and waved it over a scanner. The door clicked open. Then he stood aside and let Bennings and Jordan pass by him. They found themselves in an eight-foot-wide corridor that extended more than 100 feet. At 12-foot intervals down the right side were small metal doors, about two feet wide and a foot tall, all of them mounted about two thirds of the way up the wall. Each door was hinged at the top with a knob and a lock mechanism at the bottom.

Jordan walked up to the first door and tried to pull it open, but it wouldn't budge. He pulled harder, again with no luck.

"Here, let me give it a shot," Bennings said. He pulled a hunting knife out of his backpack and slid it underneath the bottom of the door. He pulled up, using the knife as a lever.

Crack! The lock gave way, and the door broke free. Bennings pulled the door up, and both of them stood in silence at what they saw below. They were standing about six feet above a large room with no apparent exits. The rear wall directly across from them was made out of a thick, clear acrylic material. Off in one corner of the room was a five-by-five-foot partition, which Jordan assumed concealed a bathroom of some sort. Directly below them, sitting on a sofa and watching television, was what appeared to be a 15-year-old girl.

The girl glanced up at Bennings and Jordan and asked, "Is it time for my food?"

"How long have you been in there?" Jordan asked.

The girl, suddenly realizing that there were two strange faces peering at her though the opening, ran toward them, face upturned, and said, "I don't know. Can you get me out of here? Please!"

Before either of them could answer, Bennings heard Riggs through his walkie-talkie saying, "You guys better get the hell out of there! All the guards just turned and ran back inside."

Bennings looked down the hall and said, "Damn it, Shulman's gone. He must have told them we were in here. We gotta move. Now."

"But…"

"No 'buts.' If we die in here, nobody's gonna be able to help these people. Come on, follow me!"

Bennings and Jordan tore down the hallway and back into the room. When they got there, all they found was a solid wall where the elevator had been.

Jordan looked at Bennings and said, "The son of a bitch trapped us in here."

Bennings, glancing up at the windows, said, "Maybe not. If we can get up to those windows, maybe we can rappel down the outside of the building."

Bennings reached into his backpack, pulled out a hammer, and said, "Watch this!" Then he used the hammer to smash a hole into the wall beneath the windows about three feet off the ground. Keeping the hammer in his hand, he used the hole as a toehold, pushed up, and slammed the hammer into the wall higher up. This time, he held onto the hammer with one hand while he used it as a fulcrum to swing his body up to the window ledge.

Jordan looked up and asked, "What about me, monkey man?"

"Use the toeholds, and then grab my hand. I'll get you up here."

Jordan took a running start, and using his momentum, caught both toeholds before grabbing Bennings's outstretched hand. Bennings pulled Jordan up, allowing Jordan to use his free hand to grab onto the ledge. With Jordan safely on the ledge, Bennings pulled some nylon twine out of his backpack and, as he tied it around one of the window cranks said, "This stuff is strong as hell. Open the window and let's get outta here."

Twenty seconds later, two armed guards flew out of the elevator into an empty lab. Bennings and Jordan were already in the food truck.

Jordan started up the truck as Bennings asked, "What about Benny? We can't just leave him here!"

From the back of the truck, they heard, "No worries. I'm back here. When I saw the guards flying in, I decided my best bet was to wait out here."

Jordan smiled and said, "Good call. Now get up here and drive. We'll hide in the back."

Five minutes later, they were moving safely down the road, on their way back to Milledgeville.

CHAPTER 20

MOLLY HAD HIT the road early, driving from Ithaca to New York City to attend Heather Warring's 1 p.m. political rally at Madison Square Garden. When she found out that the media was hyping the rally as a way to meet the future President and also to see her daughter, she had used her new on campus mini-celebrity status as Jesse Warring's best friend to get one of the complimentary tickets made available to Cornell. The downside: Molly's ticket was more than 30 rows back from the stage.

For the first 45 minutes of the rally, Molly listened as Heather Warring outlined all the great things she was going to do for the country as the next President. There would be free tuition for all college students, absolution of outstanding student loans, universal health care for all, and the staged elimination of fossil fuels.

Then, she switched gears and called her daughter on stage. With Blue standing by the podium, candidate Warring recounted how she had rescued poor Jessie as young child, raised her with love, and set her on a course to great success as a young woman who would smash every glass ceiling that men had ever put in her way—along with thousands of other young women. Nothing was going to stop the young women of America from taking their collective places at the top of corporate America. From that vantage point, they would eliminate profits as the driving motive behind capitalism and replace it with compassion and equality for all as they painted America green. Then, to rousing cheers, Heather turned the podium over to Jessie Warring, stepping a few feet aside.

As always, Jessie didn't waver from the speech her mother and her handlers had prepared for her. She delivered it with all of the appropriate, orchestrated emotion. She was articulate, gracious, and, of course, beautiful. As she reached the end of her speech, she segued into a new topic that Heather Warring had personally prepared for the occasion. Jessie talked about poor little Peanut, a young girl who had lived in one of WWA's foster homes, developed lymphoma, and was taken in by Heather Warring to ensure she got the proper treatment.

At Jessie's cue, Peanut walked on stage, her head bowed, her body shaking. She went up to Heather Warring and gave her a quick, scripted hug, and then moved to Jessie's side and held on tight. As Heather Warring watched, the crowd jumped to their feet for a standing ovation as tears rolled down the cheeks of men and women alike. Heather Warring stood there with her first family, waving and smiling. *Like taking candy from a baby!*

Then, in what Fox News would later refer to as a classless and arrogant move, *Hail to the Chief,* a theme historically reserved for the President, suddenly blasted throughout the arena. Blue, Peanut, and Heather Warring stood and waved—as red, white, and blue balloons fell from the rafters. Even

Molly, from her seat 30 rows away, couldn't help but think that Heather Warring might not be as bad a person as Blue had made her out to be.

As the attendees moved toward the exits, Molly desperately tried to get Blue's attention, making it all the way down to the fifth row before a security guard blocked her. She called Blue's name at the top of her voice, but with the music still blaring and security surrounding the Warrings, Molly didn't have a chance. She would have to return to Ithaca without getting a chance to talk to her friend.

Back stage, the security team was directing the Warrings, Peanut, and Jimmy Harris toward two waiting limos parked under the building.

As they approached the cars, Heather pulled Jessie aside and said, "There's been a slight change of plans, honey. I need to stay in the city with Jimmy to meet up for cocktails and dinner with some deep-pocket contributors. I've arranged for Travis to drive you and Peanut to Teterboro Airport. You two can take the private jet back to Atlanta."

"Just the two of us?" *This isn't like her.*

"Yes. You were both so wonderful today, I've arranged for two nights in the penthouse suite at the Terrace for you guys when you get there. No mother to hound you, no security... you'll be completely on your own."

Jessie said, "I don't even know what to say. Thank you so much, Mom."

"No, thank you, honey. We've got a long campaign ahead of us. So just enjoy, both of you."

Blue saw Travis waving her over to an open car door, so she gave her mother a quick kiss on the cheek. Peanut gave Heather a polite smile, and they moved toward the car.

Just as Travis closed the door for them, Peanut glanced out the side window and caught a glimpse of Heather Warring's driver. Her face turned white, and she started to cry. Tapping on Jessie's shoulder, she pointed to Willard Lance and said, "Jessie, Jessie, that's the man who raped me!"

Jessie took Peanut in her arms and leaning forward said, "Travis, get us out of here. Right now." Then, she comforted Peanut and said, "I'm sorry. I'll make sure that you never have to see that man again."

Ten minutes later, Peanut had nodded off in the back of the car. Blue leaned forward and softly asked Travis, "Who was he—the man driving the other car? I know I've seen him around, but I don't know his name."

Travis said, "That was Willard Lance, your mom's chief of security."

"Well, you heard what Peanut said—that he raped her, back when she was in one of mom's WWA foster homes, the one in downtown Atlanta. Is that possible?"

"I don't know. But I can tell you I don't like him one bit. I shouldn't tell you this, but right after I brought you back from Atlanta, your mom made him my boss. Truth is, I think it was so he could spy on both of us."

"I'm sorry. That's my fault. I should never have run off without getting her permission first. It put you in a bad spot."

"Don't worry about it. Truth is, you're the only reason I didn't jump ship long ago."

"But what can we do about what Peanut just told me? You think I can talk to my mom about it?"

"I doubt it. For now, why don't you just keep Peanut as calm as you can and leave Lance to me. I'll think of something. I promise."

"Thanks, Travis. You're the best."

CHAPTER 21

BLUE AND PEANUT had settled into their room at the Georgian Terrace, and Peanut was asleep on the sofa. Blue left Peanut a note, and then she headed down to the concierge desk and asked to use the phone to make an outside call. The clerk, recognizing her, quickly obliged. A minute later, Blue said, "Molly, it's Blue!"

"Oh my God, I just got home from your mom's rally. You and your friend Peanut were great."

"Why didn't you track us down?"

"I tried. But I couldn't get within 100 yards!"

"Sorry. But forget about today. I called to see if there was any chance you could catch a quick flight to Atlanta. I just got a two-day hall pass from my mother, so it's just Peanut and me. We're staying in the penthouse at the Georgian Terrace, and we've got plenty of room!"

"Heck, I just finished the drive back to Ithaca, and you're already lounging in Atlanta. Must be nice. As for flying down there, I'd love to, but I've got an important thesis due in a couple of days."

"Oh! That's too bad. I was really hoping you could join us."

Molly heard the disappointment in Blue's voice and asked, "What's the matter? Something's bothering you. I can tell."

"Nothing, I guess, but this isn't like my mom—letting us fly here on her private jet and then letting me stay here for two days without any security."

"Hey. Maybe she's changing. She sure sounded great on stage today."

"Maybe, maybe not."

"Okay, tell you what. I'll check the flights and see if I can fly down there tomorrow. In the meantime, would you feel better if I tell my dad and Mr. Bennings where you are? They could get there in a couple of hours."

"I don't know. I'm probably worrying too much. I'll let you go now, but keep me posted. Love you, Mols."

"Love you, too. Stay safe and enjoy!"

Blue thanked the receptionist, and then headed up the elevator. When she got back to the suite and opened the door, she heard the TV in Peanut's room. She walked through the sitting room and gently knocked on the door.

"Come in," came the response.

Blue found Peanut in bed with the covers pulled up to her chin.

Blue walked over, sat down on the bed, and asked, "Hey there, sleepy head, what are you watching?"

Peanut smiled and said, "Nothing. I was just waiting for you to come back. I want to talk to you." Then, Peanut turned off the TV.

Blue smiled, gently stroked Peanut's hair away from her eyes, and said, "Sure thing. What is it you wanna talk about?"

"Me and you."

"Okay, what about me and you?"

"I want you to know that I appreciate all you've done for me. I'm lucky to know you."

Blue laughed and said, "Get out of here, girlfriend. I'm the lucky one—not you. Now stop it before I hit you with a pillow. How about we call room service for some ice cream or something?"

"No, I'm serious. Please, listen to me for a minute."

Blue nodded, settled down, and said, "Okay. I'm listening."

"Good. Because I want you to know just how special a friend you are. Growing up, I was always sick. My mom used to call me the runt of the litter, at least when she was sober. After she died, I kept getting shuffled around from foster home to foster home. Then I met you. Do you remember when you came to visit the WWA home?"

"Of course. I remember it like it was yesterday."

"Well, I do, too. You spent over an hour with me that day. It meant so much to me that you seemed interested in what I had to say."

"That's because I was interested. You're a really cool kid!"

"Then you came back again, and you even brought me some homemade cookies."

Yup. Isn't that when I gave you your nickname?"

"Yes, it is!"

Peanut started struggling as tears formed in her eyes. "Well, you're the only one who actually cares about me." She broke down crying as Blue took her in her arms, and they cried together.

After a few minutes, Blue pulled back, mustered

up a smile, and said, "Look! That's all in the past. Going forward, you and I are gonna rule the world. The doctors say that you're almost in remission now, and as soon as that lymphoma crap is under control, watch out!"

Peanut, her head down on her chest, gave the slightest nod. Blue used her finger to pull her chin up and, looking in Peanut's eyes, said, "Hey, you! Am I right or not?"

Peanut wiped some more tears away, cracked a small smile, and said, "Yeah, you're right."

"Good. Now that we've got that settled, I'm calling down for some goodies. What would you like? Ice cream, cookies, what is it, partner?

"Think I could get a peanut sundae?"

"Ha, ha! You bet you can. I should have known!"

CHAPTER 22

THE AIR SMELLED fresher than usual, and the sky looked a little bluer. It was a 65-degree day with very little humidity when Blue and Peanut stepped out the door of the Georgian Terrace. Blue looked at Peanut and said, "Today is our day. No, check that. Today is *your* day. Where do you wanna go?"

"How about the aquarium? I love that place."

"Perfect. After that, if you want, we can walk over to the World of Coca-Cola.

"I'd like that. Oh, wait! Aren't you worried that people will recognize you?"

"Heck, no. I'm not famous. Besides, take a look—no makeup, got my Braves hat on, and I'm wearing these things," Blue said as she wiggled her sunglasses. "Come on! It's so nice out, let's walk down the street for a bit before we hail a cab."

Blue took Peanut's hand, and Peanut looked up at her with a big smile on her face.

It's the happiest I've ever seen her! Blue thought.

****

Two hours later, Blue and Peanut walked out of the aquarium and headed toward the Coca-Cola building. Peanut paused, looked at Blue, and asked,

"Could we maybe do this tomorrow instead? I'm a bit tired."

"Oh, I'm sorry. I wasn't thinking. Tell you what..." Then Blue felt her phone vibrating in her purse, and she said, "Hold on a sec. I got a phone call."

She pulled her iPhone out of her purse and saw it was Molly.

H'mm. I probably should have told her not to call me on this thing. Blue thought.

"Hey there, Mols. Surprised you're calling me... uh, you know.... What's up?"

"I know. I tried the hotel first but needed to tell you that I can't get down there. All the flights are either booked, or they cost a small fortune."

"Oh. Okay. Peanut and I will just have to make do without you. But you're missing out on some beautiful weather."

"Oh, great, now you're gonna rub it in."

Blue looked at Peanut and continued, "Yeah, and if Peanut's up for it, we're about to head over to her favorite restaurant—the Varsity."

Peanut got a huge smile on her face as she nodded her head and said, "Yes!"

On the other end of the phone, Molly said, "Well, I'll be there in spirit anyway, just like my painting where the little girl's being watched over by an angel. You know that one, don't you?"

"Of course, I do." Blue said, while thinking, *Molly's dad must be on the way!*

"Good. You take care, and I'm sure an angel will watch over you as well. Love you. Say hello to Peanut for me. I can't wait to meet her."

"I will. I love you, too. Bye now."

Blue put her phone away, looked at Peanut, and said, "Molly says hi. She really wants to meet you."

"I'd like to meet her, too. I'm sure she's really nice."

"Oh, yeah. You two are gonna really hit it off. Now let me get ahold of Uber, and we'll head over to The Varsity."

CHAPTER 23

ON THE THIRD level of the parking deck at the Georgian Terrace, sitting inside a faded red, rusted-out 1999 Chevy Silverado pickup truck, a middle-aged man with a foreign accent held his phone to his ear said, "Okay, I got it. The Varsity. On my way." A minute later, he put the truck in gear and headed down the exit ramp.

About the same time, Jordan answered his cell phone from the passenger's seat of the Toyota and asked Molly, who was on the other end, "Did you find out where she is?"

"I did. She's headed to the Varsity for lunch. Peanut, the girl who's fighting cancer, is with her."

"Good. I'd say we're about a half-hour out on I-20. We'll head straight there and check in on them. Molly, please be careful. I'll explain later, but there are some very dangerous people who may be out to harm us. Do you have a friend you could stay with for a while?"

"Dad, I'm not a kid anymore."

"Listen, Molly. I'm dead serious. Isn't there anyone up there? Wait! I have an idea. Why don't you go and stay at Nana's for a few days? Just don't tell anyone where you're going."

"But, Dad. I've got classes here and things to do."

"Molly, I'm begging you. Please?"

"Wow. You're serious, aren't you?"

"I am."

"Okay. I'll do it. But just for a couple of days."

"Thank you, pumpkin. Get packed and get out of there, now! I love you."

"Love you too, Dad."

Bennings glanced at Jordan and said, "Pumpkin! You still call her pumpkin?"

Jordan smiled and said, "Just keep your eyes on the road. We're headed to the Varsity in downtown Atlanta."

CHAPTER 24

THE VARSITY RESTAURANT is near Georgia Tech, in the middle of downtown Atlanta. It's big, taking up two city blocks crammed in between the busy streets and highways surrounding the city. With its fifties vibe and drive-up carhop service, it's popular with both tourists and locals, especially the college crowd.

Rather than pulling into the parking deck, the Uber driver pulled up to the entrance on the east side of the building so he'd have a quick exit back onto Spring Street. As Blue and Peanut prepared to hop out of the car, he glanced around and said, "You guys better walk straight in. Looks like they just re-painted the handicapped spots along both sides."

He was right. The parking spaces to both sides of the restaurant's glass entrance doors had been taped off. Blue and Peanut could smell the fresh blue paint.

Blue thanked the driver, and she walked with Peanut between the yellow cement pillars protect-ing the glass entranceway from errant drivers and into the restaurant. Inside, Blue and Peanut made their way to the restaurant's 60-foot-long service counter, chose a line to stand in, and waited to place their order behind the usual large lunch crowd. A few minutes later, it was their turn. Peanut ordered her favorite meal—a chili cheese dog and a vanilla milkshake. Blue went for the pimento cheese sandwich with fries and a Coke.

As Blue and Peanut waited for their food, the Silverado pickup truck pulled around the side of the building where the girls had been dropped off and parked on the far side of the parking lot. The driver backed the truck into a parking space, giving him a clear view of who was coming and going from the restaurant.

Minutes later, Bennings and Jordan pulled into the Varsity's main parking deck and parked on the upper level. Jordan looked over at Bennings and said, "You wait here. I'll see if I can find them." A few minutes later, Jordan pulled out his cell phone, called Bennings, and said, "Change of plans. I could use your help in here. This place is huge."

"Okay. Be right there."

No sooner had Jordan hung up when he spotted Blue and Peanut. They were weaving their way through the lunch crowd toward the exit. By the time the girls reached the doors, Jordan, gently sliding past customers, had closed to within 20 feet of them. He watched as Blue opened the door, held it for Peanut, and then followed her outside. As the door closed behind them, Jordan saw the red truck pull out of its parking spot and move past the doors and out of sight.

What the— I know that truck!

It was older than the one that Taylor Riggs drove, but it had his company's logo on the side. A few seconds later, he heard the unmistakable sound of a V-8 engine revving higher and higher, and then the squealing of tires. He charged out the restaurant door, screaming "Blue! Get back!"

But he was a fraction of a second too late. Blue and Peanut had just walked past the cement pillars, and they were standing directly in the truck's path. It was almost on top of them. Blue turned toward the sound of Jordan's voice, grabbed hold of Peanut's hand, and jumped backward, pulling Peanut with all her strength. Blue had barely cleared the pillars when Peanut's hand was ripped from her own to the sickening sound of a loud thump. It was the sound of the cold steel of a truck's front grill and bumper smashing into human flesh and bones. As Blue hit the ground, her hat and sunglasses falling off,, Peanut's body was spinning through the air like a rag doll. Seconds later, it hit the pavement with a dull thud, some 20 feet away. The truck never stopped. It flew out onto Spring Street and quickly disappeared.

As Jordan ran toward Blue, Bennings spotted him through a crowd of onlookers. He pushed past them and ran outside. He saw Jordan tending to Blue, and then spotted Peanut's crumpled body on the other side of the parking lot. He ran over, knelt beside her, and placed two fingers on her wrist, feeling for a pulse. But he knew what death looked like, and all signs of life had already left her shattered little body. He gently closed her eyes as a bystander ran up to help.

Bennings looked at the bystander and said, "Please, get me a coat, a blanket—something to cover her. She's gone." Bennings's head dropped to his chest, and a tear fell to the ground.

Spectators filled the doorway as Jordan held Blue's head in his lap and said, "Blue, Blue, are you alright? It's me, Jordan."

Blue's eyes blinked open. Dazed and disoriented, she tried to sit up. Jordan put his arm around her shoulders to help her and again he asked, "Blue, are you alright?"

Blue's eyes came into focus, and she looked at Jordan and said, "Uh, yes, I think so. What? Oh my God, where's Peanut! Where's Peanut?"

Jordan looked over and saw Bennings covering Peanut with a blanket. Their eyes met, and Bennings shook his head. Jordan turned back to Blue and said, "I'm so sorry. She's gone."

"No, no, she can't be!" Blue struggled to her feet and tried to break free as Jordan held her and said, "Please, please don't."

Blue pulled away and staggered across the parking lot. When she reached Bennings, he tried to shield her from Peanut's body, but she screamed, "No! I have to see her." She ripped free of Bennings's hold. With trembling hands, she knelt next to Peanut and slowly pulled back the blanket. Her body was shattered, but her face looked like that of a sleeping child—one lost in a peaceful dream. Blue, her body now convulsing and tears pouring down her cheeks, said, "Peanut, I'm so sorry. I was supposed to protect you. Please, please, can you ever forgive me?"

Jordan walked over to Blue, knelt down, put his arm around her, and said, "Blue, it's not your fault. You did everything you could."

She turned to him and yelled, "No! No, I didn't.

I'm the one who put her in harm's way." Then Blue buried her head in Jordan's shoulder and cried. As Bennings pulled the blanket back up over Peanut's face, sirens could be heard in the distance.

CHAPTER 25

BLUE WAS STILL answering questions for the investigating officer when Peanut's body was being loaded into the back of a coroner's van. Behind the police tape, local camera crews were milling around, searching for eyewitnesses among the crowd. Bennings and Jordan, having given their statements to police earlier, watched from a distance.

Bennings, seeing the coroner's van pull out, asked , "Now what? We both know who's responsible, and we can't do a damned thing about it. What about Blue? Her own fucking mother just tried to kill her."

Jordan said, "Yeah, and there's more to it than that."

"Really?"

"I don't know if you heard what I told the officer, but the truck that hit Peanut had Taylor Riggs's company logo on it. I saw that same truck on the news coverage from the protest that Riggs helped us to orchestrate out at Warring Pharmaceuticals. It was Eddie's truck—Riggs's goofy friend. He's the guy who pulled Heather Warring's effigy out from the back of that truck and set it on fire."

Bennings inhaled deeply, then exhaled, and said, "That bitch puts out a hit out on her own daughter, and then sets up Eddie and his radical gun-loving friends to take the fall. I can already hear the news coverage."

"Yup. And since dead men tell no tales, you know that when they find that truck, they're gonna find Eddie's body behind the wheel."

Neither man said anything for a couple of minutes. Then Jordan looked at Bennings and said, "You know, I don't think that even Heather Warring could have pulled this off without some outside help."

Bennings nodded and said, "I was thinking the same thing."

Jordan looked at Bennings and asked, "Where does that put us? Are we next?"

Bennings's face suddenly lit up, and he said, "Maybe not. Come here, and follow my lead."

Jordan watched as Bennings made a beeline toward Brent Keaster and a GNN camera crew.

Oh shit. Here we go! Jordan thought.

Keaster had just cut short an interview with a tourist who claimed he saw the whole thing when Bennings approached him and said, "Hey, you, Mr. GNN! You want a real eyewitness? If you do, he's right over there!" as he pointed to Jordan.

Bennings continued, "He's a good friend of Jessie Warring, and he's the one who saved her life. In fact, I think it might have been the governor herself who sent him out here to protect Jessie after learning that someone was going to try to murder her daughter."

Jordan almost swallowed his tongue as Keaster pivoted toward him and waved over his camera crew. With lights flashing in Jordan's face, Keaster looked at the camera and said, "We're back again live at the Varsity in downtown Atlanta. I've just been informed that this man is an eye-witness to this tragedy, and he saved Jessie Warring's life."

Then sticking a microphone in Jordan's face, he asked, "Sir, can you tell us what happened here today?"

Throwing Bennings a look, Jordan said, "Yeah, I guess so. A faded red truck, a Chevy I think, came flying down the side of the building, aiming directly at... um Jessie and Peanut."

"The deceased's name is Peanut?"

Damn.

"No, that was her nickname. She and Jessie were good friends. When I saw the truck, I yelled out. Jessie turned and jumped behind the cement pillars near the doorway as the truck flew by. She tried to pull Peanut back to safety, but the truck, well, you know what happened after that."

"Do you think this was an accident, or an intentional attempt to inflict harm?"

"Oh, it was definitely intentional."

"I've been told that you were asked by the governor to come here to protect Jessie—something to do with death threats she had received. Is that true?"

Jordan glanced over at Bennings who was off camera and saw him mouthing "yes."

Jordan looked back at Keaster and said, "No. I was asked to come here, but not by the governor. I've never met her. I've never even talked to her."

"Then who asked you?"

"I'd rather not say."

"Well, can you at least tell us what they said?"

Jordan hesitated, but he saw Bennings violently nodding his head and egging him on.

At that point, Jordan took a deep breath and gave in to Bennings's prods.

"Actually, I will tell you. Someone very close to Jessie called me and said that she was in extreme danger, that the Deep State wanted her terminated, and then they asked me to help."

"The Deep State? You don't really believe that. Do you?"

With Bennings flashing a smile and giving him a big thumbs up, Jordan looked right into the camera and said, "You're damn right I do. The Deep State is real, and they are in the process of destroying this entire country. Now are you finished?"

"Just about. I didn't catch your name."

"That's because you didn't ask. My name is Jordan Nichols, and if you're not done yet, I sure as hell am."

As Jordan turned and walked away, the audience watching Keaster's broadcast in the comfort of their homes heard him wrap up by saying, "Obviously, Mr. Nichols is a bit disoriented, perhaps he's still in a *deep state* of shock. I may not know everything, but I doubt that the Deep State drives old pickup trucks."

Keaster suddenly adjusted his earbud and said, "In fact, wait a second. I've just been told that the police have located the truck involved in today's hit and run. It was found on a rural road about 15 miles out of town. The driver was found dead from a self-inflicted gun-shot wound. In the coming days, I'm sure we will find out why he would have wanted to do such a horrible thing. And while we at GNN never speculate, one can't help but wonder if it was indeed a right-wing extremist group that perpetrated this terrible act. Now, back to the studio."

Jordan walked over to Bennings and asked, "What the fuck was that all about? You just had me sign my own death warrant on national TV!"

"No, I'm pretty sure I did just the opposite."

"Really?"

"Yes, really. Question! Do you think that Blue will be willing to leave here with us tonight, and not attend Peanut's funeral?"

"No way."

"Of course not! Which means that we've already lost our only chance to take Blue with us and sneak out of Dodge. I guarantee that Heather Warring is on her way here, right now!"

"What did my little interview have to do with any of that?"

"It bought us time, especially the part about the Deep State. The whole world is about to hear that some right-wing redneck killed Peanut and tried to kill Blue, and now he's dead. So, thanks to your little crazy man statement about the Deep State, if Blue or either of us get killed, you're not gonna look so crazy, are you? The way I see it, the bad guys now have to wait a while before they kill us—at least until things calm down a bit."

"Thank you. I feel so much better now. I'm alive and crazy, rather than dead and validated."

"Something like that... but stop complaining. After the funeral, we'll figure out a way to grab Blue and head to my safe house. From there, we'll plan our next move."

"Did you just say 'my safe house'?"

"Of course. When you work undercover for over 10 years breaking up international drug rings, it pretty much goes with the territory."

"Yeah, I guess it would."

A chopper could be heard approaching from a distance. Bennings looked out beyond the crime scene and saw that the police had West Street blocked off. He looked at Jordan and asked, "You wanna stick around? Looks like the *gov* is about to land and give her little girl a big hug and shed some fake tears for the cameras."

Jordan nodded and said, "You know what, I do. I want to look her in the eye and give her a chance to thank me on national TV."

Bennings smiled and asked, "I wonder if she'll ask you about the Deep State?"

"Shut up. Just shut the hell up."

CHAPTER 26

IT WAS ANOTHER beautiful fall day when Peanut was laid to rest. Heather Warring, taking advantage of the photo op, had arranged to have her buried at noon with as much pomp and circumstance as one can bring to the death of an unknown orphan. The cemetery chosen was Memory Hill in Milledgeville. It's on the National Register of Historic Places and is the eternal home to many of Georgia's antebellum and post-antebellum legislators as well as author Flannery O'Connor and the University of Georgia's first football coach.

The service was held at the gravesite, providing the convenience of one-stop shopping for the press. In fact, there were almost as many reporters and cameramen there as mourners, in spite of the fact that Heather Warring trotted out plenty of orphans from the Atlanta WWA foster home and state Senators and Congressmen. In reality, the only people truly mourning Peanut's death that day were Blue, Jordan, and Bennings.

When the service concluded, Heather Warring remained by the grave, talking to reporters and posing for pictures. State troopers and several secret service agents stood in the background watching. The situation unfolded exactly how Bennings and Jordan had anticipated.

As her mother talked to the press, Blue walked with Travis toward the family limo, which was idling nearby. Jordan and Bennings walked behind them, keeping a respectful distance. When Travis opened the door for Blue, Jordan and Bennings pulled their Glocks out from under their suit jackets and rushed the car. Jordan shoved Blue into the backseat and jumped in beside her. Bennings yanked Travis away from the car door and punched him in the stomach. With Travis buckled over in pain, Bennings ran around to the driver's side, jumped in, and took off down the road. As Travis lay on the ground, he watched the car peel away—and smiled. The fake kidnapping had been perfectly executed. Travis had worked it out with Jordan the day before over lunch at Bully's.

Inside the car, Jordan yelled, "Go. Go. Go!" as Bennings flew down the street. Looking back through the rear window, Jordan saw the state police run to their cars and take up pursuit as the secret service men in attendance pulled out their cell phones.

Jordan, staying focused on the rear window said, "Dude, we've got maybe three or four minutes max before they've got eyes in the sky. After that, we're screwed." Then, turning to Blue, Jordan said, "Remember, if this goes bad, you've been kidnapped. You got that?"

Jordan's harsh tone startled Blue, and the magnitude of what had just occurred hit her. She nodded her head and said, "Yes, sir."

As Bennings slid through a hard right turn onto RT 24, the tires squealed, and Jordan crashed against Blue in the backseat. Bennings slammed the pedal to the floor and yelled, "They're gonna catch us within a couple of miles, so I sure as shit hope he's there!"

"He will be," Jordan said.

Bennings saw the pickup truck at a crossroad ahead and said, "Thank you, sweet Jesus, I see him."

As soon as the limo flew through the intersection, Taylor Riggs pulled his truck and landscape trailer across the road and stopped. Inside the truck, Riggs reached down and pulled the hood release. Then he jumped out, popped the hood, and yanked off the radiator hose he had loosened earlier that morning.

By the time the two state police cars reached Riggs's truck, steam was pouring out from under the hood. One of the troopers jumped out and screamed, "Move that truck, you son of a bitch."

Riggs smiled and said, "I'm sorry, officer. The engine just crapped out on me." Then, under his breath, he said, *That's for you, Eddie.*

Back inside the limo, Bennings glanced in the rearview mirror and said, "Okay, one problem solved. Now for the next one."

A quarter mile down the road, Bennings slammed on the brakes and took a hard right turn onto a small dirt access road surrounded by huge Georgia pine trees. No sooner had they passed under the canopy of trees when Jordan said, " I hear it. I hear a chopper."

Bennings stopped the car, rolled down the driver's side window, and listened as the chopper flew overhead and kept moving down the highway. No one said a word. Bennings rolled the window up and drove slowly forward, careful not to kick up any dust until he reached a small fishing hole. There was an old SUV sitting next to it. He pulled the limo off the road, keeping it under the pine trees, hopped out, and sticking his head back in the car said, "Get out, and wait here. I'll bring the truck over."

Bennings ran about 20 yards to the black, 2010 Chevy Tahoe, jumped in, fired it up, and pulled up next to the limo. Blue got in the back as Jordan jumped in the passenger's seat, scooping up two Georgia Bulldog caps off the seat before he sat down. He handed one to Bennings and put the other one on as he got in the truck.

As Bennings slowly drove back down the dirt road, Blue leaned over the front seat and asked, "Where did you get this thing?"

"We bought it over in Macon," Jordan said. "We paid cash and then switched the plates."

Bennings said, "Hey, Blue, do you have any electronics on you? Cellphone, ear buds, anything?"

"No, nothing."

"You're absolutely sure? Not even a watch?"

"Positive. Travis told me to leave everything at home."

"Okay. Then do me a favor and huddle down on the floor for a while. Just in case."

As Bennings neared the main road, they heard police sirens. He stopped about 50 feet back and watched as two state cop cars flew past and disappeared up the highway. Bennings smiled, looked at Jordan, and said, "Guess we'll go the other way."

Then he pulled onto the highway and took a left, backtracking toward town.

Jordan nodded and asked, "Where is this safe house of yours? You still haven't told me."

"In the mountains in North Carolina. We'll be there in about six or seven hours." Blue, on the floor of the Tahoe, curled up, and closed her eyes and slept—for the next six hours.

****

The gentle rolling hills to the north of Atlanta were far behind them as the Tahoe moved along a back road in the Appalachian Mountains of North Carolina. Bennings and Jordan were watching the sun starting to disappear behind the mountain peaks when they heard Blue say, "Wow, that is really beautiful."

Jordan turned and said, "Hi there, sleepy head. How are you feeling?"

I'm good, I guess. But I'm scared to death for you guys. Why is all of this happening?"

Jordan turned around, smiled, and said, "We don't have all the answers yet, but what we do know is that if it weren't for you, we wouldn't have a chance to keep Heather Warring and whomever she's working for from destroying this country. At least you've given us a fighting chance."

Blue sarcastically said, "Yahoo! The Three Musketeers versus the Deep State, coming to a theater near you!"

Bennings said, "What did you just say?"

Blue said, "I was just kidding. We're like the Three Musketeers."

"Not that part, the part about *coming to a theater near you*. I think you're on to something!"

Just then, as they rounded a bend on the mountain road, Jordan pointed to a small black object in the sky, positioned between their car and the setting sun. He said, "Look. I think that's a helicopter, just over the ridge—where the sun's setting. Is he tracking us?"

Bennings, squinting to block the sun's rays, picked it up, but just as he did, the helicopter tilted forward and sped off, disappearing behind the ridge. Bennings and Jordan exchanged glances as Jordan said, "Just nervous I guess."

Bennings said, "Yeah. Let's hope so."

CHAPTER 27

THE LAST ROAD they traveled was nothing more than loose gravel over a dirt base, cut into the side of a mountain with steep drop-offs on the driver's side and rising terrain on the passengers side. The trees were dense, mostly poplar, with some hickory as well. Half the leaves were already on the ground. It had recently rained, leaving some slick surfaces and nervous moments as they navigated the tight road.

After about 20 miles, there was a small cut-out where the road widened. Bennings slowed down, pulled the Tahoe to the side of the road, and said, "Jordan, come with me. Blue, stay put. We'll be right back."

Jordan walked with Bennings about 20 feet up the road where Bennings bent down, grabbed onto the trunk of a rotting out tree that was lying parallel to the road, and turned it 45 degrees to the side. As he pulled it across the bed of leaves, Jordan saw that there was a narrow dirt road underneath, running directly up the slope. He said, "Hey, let me help you with that."

Bennings, dropping the tree back to the ground, said, "No need. Just stay here and put it back in place after I drive past. Oh, and try to spread the leaves around when you're done. Make it look as natural as possible."

"Okay, will do."

After Jordan was back inside the Tahoe, Bennings said, "Hold on now, both of you. This is where the four-wheel drive is gonna come in handy, especially with wet leaves all over the place."

As Bennings drove forward, the slope quickly steepened. The truck spun and kicked its way up the hill, at one point suddenly sliding sideways and banging against a tree on the passenger's side. Jordan flinched as Blue held onto the grab handle above the rear door. Bennings glanced at both of them with a grin. He'd done it before and knew the outcome in advance. Just as the incline increased to about 65 degrees, the terrain suddenly flattened out. As the nose of the truck dropped, Jordan and Blue saw a small, run-down wooden clapboard cabin in front of them. If it had ever been painted, you couldn't tell. There was a rotting wooden porch across the front, a door in the center of the building, and a single window to the right.

Bennings shut down the motor, turned, and asked, "What do you think? It was built by moonshiners, sometime during Prohibition."

Blue gave a tentative smile and said, "It's uh, certainly remote."

Jordan nodded and said, "Yeah, they must have cleared the land with nothing more than dynamite, pick-axes, and shovels. How the hell did you ever come across it?"

"The FBI had some perks. Just so happens that the government confiscated it for back income taxes. I got it for all of $2,000."

As they stepped out of the Tahoe, Blue smiled and said, "I think you got taken."

Bennings laughed and said, "Well, let me show you around. It has a certain charm."

Inside, Jordan and Blue found a 20-foot deep by 30-foot wide room rising up to an open beamed ceiling. Spanning the length of the entire rear wall was a five-foot deep loft, accessed by a hand-built stairway tied into the left wall of the cabin. Under the stairway and loft were storage closets that spanned half of the room from the left side. From there on over was a rudimentary kitchen that included four feet of base cabinets covered in faded red linoleum, a self-standing sink with no faucet next to a water cooler, a propane camp stove sitting on a table, and a mini-fridge. The fridge, along with about 10 light bulbs that were screwed into porcelain bases mounted to walls throughout the cabin, were powered by a small propane generator sitting outside the cabin.

Centered on the right-hand wall was a wood-fired, potbelly stove. It was the only source of heat, and its round black chimney rose several feet above the stove before turning and disappearing through a hole in the wall. Placed around the fireplace were four plastic white chairs—the cheap, stackable kind sold at big box stores.

As Jordan and Blue took it all in, Bennings picked up a mouse trap with a dead mouse in it and said, "Got him," before tossing the mouse, trap and all, into a nearby garbage pail. Then he pointed to the loft and said, "Up there, that's where we'll sleep, single file along the wall. The bedding's already up there."

Blue glanced around and said, "And uh, exactly where's the bathroom?"

Bennings smiled and said, "Sorry about that. But it's called *the great outdoors* for a reason." Pointing to a peg by the door, he said, "I usually keep a roll of toilet paper on that peg over there. I'll have to get a fresh roll out of the closet. Oh, and a simple word of advice, you want to head down the hill, below the cabin. You know…gravity and all of that. And there's a shovel on the porch. I run a clean B&B."

Blue said, "Oh my God! And running water?"

"Sorry, don't have that either. The sink is just used for cleaning up. But we do have the water cooler. You can draw water from that to drink, or put some in a pot to wash up outside. When it's time for a bath, there's a nice lake about a mile and a half down the trail. Water's cold, but it's crystal clear. I can show you how to get there in the morning."

"What if I don't have a bathing suit?"

"Can't help you with that either. But if you get to the lake early, you'll pretty much have it to yourself. That's what I usually do."

Blue shook her head and said, "This is nuts. I must be trapped in some sort of B-grade horror flick. Where do you keep the chainsaws?"

Bennings smiled and said, "Ah, speaking of chain saws, I need to show you guys a couple more things."

He walked to the center of the room and pulled back an old five-by-seven area rug. Cut into the floorboards underneath was a trap door. Bennings lifted the door and said, "Check this out."

As Jordan and Blue looked over Bennings's shoulder, he asked, "See the steps? They lead to a tunnel that runs out the back—slopes up the mountain for a good 150 feet. The moonshiners must have put it in. Not only gave them an escape route, but just over the ridge of the mountain is where they kept their still. I found some remnants of it last summer when I came down here for a long weekend."

Jordan said, "What kind of shape is the tunnel in?"

"Surprisingly good. I've done some minor repairs, but the guys who built it did a heck of a job shoring it up with beams and corrugated aluminum. Besides, it only runs about a foot below ground. Up top, it exits right between two strategically placed mountain laurel. As Bennings closed the trap door, he said, "Now, let me show you something else you need to know about." He walked over to a closet underneath the stairs and opened the door to reveal two large gun safes. As he opened the first one he said, "I haven't had the time or desire to build any hidden closets, but I did manage to get these things up here, which is a story in and of itself. I'll leave this one open while were here, just in case."

Jordan, looking inside said, "Nice. I see a scoped Remington 700, an AR-15, and what's that third one, an ArmaLite AR-10?"

Bennings smiled and said, "You know your weapons. They're all ready to go, with a round in the chamber. Spare ammo's right next to them. It's all cross labeled to the specific gun, so if you're in a hurry, you won't grab the wrong box." Then, pointing to the inside of the open door, he said, "There, in those pockets, are a couple of 9mm Glocks, a SIG and...," looking at Blue he asked, "Blue, you familiar with firearms at all?"

"No, sir."

Bennings pulled a revolver out of one of the pockets, held it out, and said, "Well, then I'd recommend that you stick with this one."

Pushing it away, Blue said, "No, I don't like guns."

"Please, take it," Bennings said. "You don't have to like it. But you may need it. It's a .38 special. Five bullets. Just aim, pull the trigger, and the gun will do the rest."

Blue tentatively took the gun and held it out in front of her, taking aim at the water cooler.

Bennings gently lowered her outstretched arm and said, "Don't pull the trigger unless you mean it. It doesn't have a safety."

Blue gave him back the gun and said, "Just put it back."

Bennings put it in the top pocket inside the safe and said, "Okay. But it will be right here if you need it. Oh, and one other thing. I keep five burner phones in here. When we leave, we'll take them along. Can't be traced."

Blue nodded as Jordan glanced at the second gun safe and asked, "What's in there?"

Bennings smiled and said, "That's private stock. The heavy-duty stuff. If I need to go in there, we're all in trouble."

Jordan nodded and said, "Got it."

CHAPTER 28

THE THREE OF them were huddled around the potbelly stove, staying warm after a dinner of beef jerky, dried fruit, and a couple of beers. Bennings glanced at Jordan and Blue and said, "The way I see it, the Deep State and Heather Warring want us all dead. Well, maybe not Blue at this point, but you never know."

Jordan smiled and said, "Yup. And we're also wanted by the FBI, the Georgia state police, and God knows who else for kidnapping the governor's daughter."

Bennings smiled and said, "Yeah. Who's idea was that kidnapping thing?"

"Well, you sure as hell didn't have a better idea. Did you?"

Blue stood up and yelled, "Will you two stop it? I don't think this situation is funny at all." With tears forming in her eyes, she said, "First, I get Peanut killed. Next, it's gonna be you guys. I just know it."

Bennings and Jordan went silent, as Blue sat down sobbing.

A few minutes passed, and Jordan put his arm around Blue's shoulder and said, "Hey you, cheer up. Bennings and I, we put ourselves in this situation because we chose to. Besides, I love you, kiddo."

Bennings nodded and said, "As for me, I don't have a lot going on in my life. But I love this country, and I don't see what we're doing now any different than men and women who fight and die every day to preserve our freedom. It's what I do, and if I die in the process, can't think of a better way to go."

Another minute of silence passed before Jordan looked at Blue and asked, "Do you understand now where we're coming from?"

Wiping away a tear, Blue said, "I guess so, but if that was supposed to be a pep talk, it was really pathetic. So, whatever fate is in store for the two of you is gonna be the same for me, understood? It's gonna be the Three Musketeers till the bitter end."

Jordan raised the Bud Light he was nursing and said, "Okay then, to the Three Musketeers."

Bennings stood up and said, "On that note, I think we all need to get some sleep. I'll use the uh, outdoor bathroom facilities first." He walked to the door, opened it, and then paused. He turned back to Jordan and Blue and asked, "You hear that?"

At first, it was more of a low sonic vibration felt in the gut rather than a sound heard by the ear. But then they all heard it—the sound of a large helicopter, close by, hovering over the mountain.

Bennings said, "That's a big one. I'd say it's a Sikorsky by the sound of it."

As Bennings closed the door, Blue got up and walked toward the window to peek outside. When she reached the window, out of the corner of her eye she saw a small red dot on her blouse. She looked up and staring her in the face, directly outside the window, was a small black drone.

"Look out!" Jordan yelled.

But it was too late. There was a loud *BANG*, *CRACK*—two different sounds, milliseconds apart. The first was that of a small caliber bullet being fired, the second was the sound of the bullet hitting the window. Blue instinctively reached for her blouse, but there was no blood. The window had cracked, but it was still intact. Bennings ran to Blue and pushed her away from the window, and then retreated to the door, locking it.

Jordan ran to the open gun safe and asked, "What do you want? The AR 15?"

"No need. At least not right now. That's bullet-proof glass."

"But what if they're rappelling down from the chopper?"

"I don't think that's the plan. They're using the chopper as the command center for the drones. Look, here come some more!"

They all turned to the window to see five more black drones hovering directly outside. Jordan pulled his Glock from his side holster and ran toward Blue, who had ducked to one side of the window as Bennings remained by the door. As Jordan ran toward Blue, two more shots hit the glass, but they didn't penetrate.

"Jordan, try to stay out of sight, grab one of those chairs, and toss it past the window," Bennings said.

"Why? What are you thinking?"

"Please, just do it."

"Whatever you say!"

Jordan grabbed the closest chair and tossed it

past the window. The drones stayed in place, but they didn't fire. Bennings then said, "Now it's your turn. Run past the window."

"What! Are you nuts?"

"You'll be alright. The glass should hold."

Should?

Jordan ran past the window directly toward Bennings, and two of the three remaining drones fired at him. The glass spider cracked, but again, it held.

"What's going on?" Jordan asked.

"I think that those buzzing little bastards are using a new heat and motion technology. I was just reading about it last week. The operators up in the chopper don't have eyes on us, but the drones are programmed to respond to a combination of heat and motion."

"Really? No cameras?" Jordan asked.

"I don't think so. The computers in those things are a shit load faster and smarter than anyone watching through a camera could ever be.

"Watch this!" Bennings said, as he ran to a closet underneath the loft. The one remaining drone fired at him.

Looking out the window, Jordan said, "The others all left. Looks like they only hold one round apiece."

"Roger that," Bennings said, opening a closet door. "Keeps their weight down." He rummaged around inside the closet, until he came up holding two black rubber suits. He threw them at Jordan and said, "Here, catch!"

Jordan plucked them out of the air and asked, "Thermal suits?"

Bennings said, "Yup, I use them to scuba dive down at the lake. Put them on. It should hold in your body heat, maybe confuse their heat sensors."

As Blue and Jordan pulled on the suits, Jordan asked, "What about you?"

Bennings moved to the locked gun vault, punched in the combination, and said, "Don't worry. I've got a date with that chopper up there."

"What?"

"Check this out!" Bennings turned around holding a portable ground-to-air missile launcher.

"Holy shit, an MPADS?"

Bennings smiled and said, "You really do know your weapons." As he ran toward the trap door, he continued, "You hold down the fort in here. I'll be right back. Don't assume anything. They may be re-arming the drones with a different type of ammo, maybe even cameras since they haven't been able to penetrate our defenses."

Bennings disappeared through the trap door, pulling it down behind him.

Seconds later, a fresh group of six drones appeared at the window. One drone moved out in front of the others, lined up dead center on the window, and fired. The window held. A second drone took the same position and fired on the exact same spot. Again, the window held. When the third drone moved into position and fired, the glass shattered into a million pieces and rattled across the floor.

Blue screamed as the three remaining armed drones swarmed inside.

Jordan, standing a few feet away said, "Stay calm and don't move, no matter what. Do not move!"

The drones separated. Two of them flew up to the loft and one of them focused on the stove. They moved slowly, inspecting every inch of the room. Then, the two drones up by the loft slowly descended. One of them moved toward Jordan as the other moved toward Blue. As the drone circled Jordan, he didn't flinch. He held his focus on Blue. The drone circling her slowly moved up toward her face. She did her best to stay calm, but Jordan could see the stress building.

Shit, that's right where her body heat is escaping, Jordan thought.

Then the third drone that had been by the stove joined in. Both of them circled Blue, moving up and down. Her body began to quiver as tears filled her eyes. One of the drones positioned itself directly in front of her face. It backed off about two feet and a red light flashed on the front of the drone sending a laser beam to the middle of Blue's forehead.

Jordan screamed, "I'm right here you bastards," and lashed out with his arms. His left arm caught the drone closest to him, smashing it against the wall. The two remaining drones turned toward him as he charged toward Blue.

BANG! The first drone fired, the bullet catching Jordan in the front of his left shoulder. It spun him sideways, but as he fell to the floor, he reached out and knocked Blue to the ground, shielding her body with his own. The remaining drone moved in, lining up a kill shot. The red laser beam went on, targeting the back of Jordan's head.

FLASH!

The entire sky lit up, sending a bright flash of

light streaming through the window, a millisecond before a massive explosion rocked the entire cabin. As debris rained down from the sky, all three drones fell to the floor, lifeless.

Jordan rolled off Blue, clutching his shoulder. Blue saw the blood on her shirt, and then saw it oozing out from under Jordan's hand and screamed, "Oh my God!"

Jordan, peeking at the wound offered up a weak smile and said, "I'll be okay. We need to check on Bennings."

Before Blue could react, the trap door opened, and Bennings pulled himself up into the room. He saw Jordan holding his shoulder and said, "Shit. You alright?"

Jordan zipped the suit down to the waist with his free hand, looked at the wound, and said, "Yeah. Doesn't look like it hit an artery. Should be fine." Then, noticing a hole in the back of the thermal suit, he said, "In fact, it looks like it went clean through."

"Okay. Let's get you tended to so we can get the hell outta here."

Bennings ran for a first aid kit as Jordan smiled and said, "Yeah. You lit up the sky pretty good out there!"

****

Ten minutes later, Bennings threw a duffel bag and some weapons into the back of the Tahoe and ran back toward the cabin carrying a two-gallon plastic container of gasoline. He ran inside the cabin and worked his way back to the porch, emptying the gasoline as he went. He tossed the empty container down on the porch, threw a lit match down, and ran to the Tahoe where Jordan and Blue were waiting inside.

As they drove down the hill, Bennings watched in the rearview mirror as flames shot up from the cabin. He shook his head and said, "Damn, I really liked that place."

"Sorry," Jordan said. "Did you get everything we need?"

"Yup. It's all in the back, including a duffel bag full of odds and ends, a first aid kit, and the burner phones."

As they crept down the mountain and neared the main road, they saw headlights filtering through the trees. Then they heard sirens approaching. Bennings turned off the Tahoe's headlights and shot off the trail at an angle. He slowly maneuvered around trees and moved toward the main road before pulling to a complete stop, about 30 feet to the right of the path they had used earlier that day. He shut off the engine and watched as off to the left, an all-terrain fire vehicle with powerful halogen headlights and huge, knobby tires led the way up the mountain with two police Jeeps following right behind. Bennings waited until they moved closer to the fire, and then started the Tahoe, worked around some trees, and got it back onto the main road. A quarter mile down the mountain, he turned the headlights on and left his burning cabin behind.

A few miles down the road, Jordan looked at

Bennings and quietly said, "There's no way they could have found us that fast unless...you know."

Bennings nodded and said, "I know."

Jordan turned to the backseat and looked at Blue.

Blue looked at him and asked, "What? I told you: I did not bring any electronics with me. I swear!"

Bennings glancing in the rearview mirror asked, "Have you had any type of surgery since you've been living with the governor—a broken bone, boob job, even dental surgery?"

"No, nothing!" Oh, shit. Wait a second. I did have an emergency appendectomy a couple of years ago."

Bennings said, "Okay. Jordan, grab the flashlight from the glovebox and help Blue find where a microchip might be planted."

Jordan pulled out the flashlight, turned toward the backseat, and found Blue already sliding off her jeans. When he saw the thong she was wearing, he blushed and quickly turned away.

Blue said, "Mr. Nichols, I need the flashlight. I mean for God's sake, it's no different than a bathing suit."

Holding out the flashlight behind him without turning around, Jordan said, "Fine. You take it and feel along the sides of the scar line from the operation. Tell me if you feel anything a bit out of the ordinary—like a bump."

Blue, rubbing her finger across the scar said, "The scar feels bumpy. Is that what you mean?"

"No, that's probably just scar tissue. It would be to one side or the other."

Blue ran her fingers along both sides of the scar line. As she did, Jordan peeked back to make sure she was doing what had been asked.

He blushed again and quickly turned away saying, "I'm sorry. Just trying to help."

Blue smiled and seconds later said, "Holy crap! I do feel something. It feels like a little hard spot. It almost feels like I can move it."

Jordan said, "Okay. Turn off the flashlight and pull up your pants. We need to find a place to perform some emergency surgery."

"What?"

Jordan said, "Don't worry. We're just gonna have to make a small incision and get that chip out."

"Oh Jesus!"

When they reached the entrance to I-81, Bennings saw a truck stop on the other side and headed for it. When he reached the parking lot, he drove directly to the darkest, most remote corner and parked. Five minutes later, he was standing outside the back door of the SUV with the door open. He had a box cutter in his hand, and Jordan was standing right behind him with some gauze and a bandage. Inside, Blue was lying across the backseat with her shirt pulled up to the top of her belly button and her jeans pulled down to her knees. She was holding a towel over her eyes with one hand and putting a strangle hold on the rear door pull with the other.

Bennings leaned in and said, "Don't worry. This won't hurt too much, but you have to lie perfectly still. You got it?"

Blue said, "Yes. Just get it over with."

Bennings, using the box cutter, cut a one-inch

incision near the top of the appendectomy scar. Then, he cut two smaller ones at 90-degree angles, creating a flap of skin. He peeled back the flap, using the flat side of the box cutter blade. There, on the dermis layer of Blue's skin, was a square microchip.

Bennings's eyes lit up. He gently slipped the box cutter underneath the chip, picked it up on the blade, and said, "I got it!" Balancing it there, he backed away, allowing Jordan to lean in and put some gauze over the incision.

Jordan put the bandage over it and said, "You can look now. It's all over."

Blue opened her eyes and said, "Really? I gotta admit; it really didn't hurt that much."

Jordan laughed and said, "Good. Now pull up your pants. You're in the middle of a Truck Stop for God's sake!" as he closed the back door and stood guard outside.

Blue laughed as she sat up and squirmed around, trying to pull up her pants as she laid on the backseat.

A few minutes later, Bennings hopped back in the driver's seat as Jordan waited in the passengers seat.

Jordan looked at him and asked, "All set?"

Bennings nodded and said, "Yup. Found an unlocked truck. That chip will soon be on its way somewhere else."

CHAPTER 29

FIFTEEN MILES DOWN the road, Blue was sound asleep in the backseat. Jordan, looking straight ahead as if he was talking to himself, asked, "What do we really know about the Deep State?"

Bennings glanced over and said, "We know that their real name is the Guild. We know they're a huge international organization with a governing council that controls most of the money and military might in the world, and they seem to be able to control our elections at will. Oh, and then there's the *end game* they are planning, which is supposed to include violence, unemployment, and all sorts of other bad shit."

"I'm betting that it's all gonna start as soon as Warring's lab work is done," Jordan said. "That's when all the Guild's members will have their magic pill, or whatever it is, to live forever. Maybe they'll let us mortals battle it out, or maybe they'll just unleash the latest and greatest disease on us all while they sit in their mansions with their vaccines and watch some of us die. You know, like a controlled kill on animal populations when they get out of hand."

Bennings said, "Wow! And I thought I was cynical. You really think it's gonna play out that way?"

"It has to. The Deep State can't share the gift of

immortality with the masses. Earth's resources would be overwhelmed within 50 years—maybe less. In fact, this immortality shit explains a whole boatload of things that have already gone down."

"Like what?"

"How about climate change? Haven't you ever wondered why there's been such an intense focus on a theoretical problem that's hundreds, maybe even thousands of years in the future? Don't get me wrong, I care about our environment as much as the next guy, but sorry, it's not human nature to obsess about something that far out in the future unless..."

Bennings finished the sentence for him, "Yeah, unless you plan to be around to enjoy that future."

"Exactly. And now the pandemics, mobs ransacking entire cities with the police ordered to stand by and watch, and finally, the big push to take away our guns. It's all part of the plan. They want to destroy our economic foundation, weaken our will by pitting us against each other, and finally, take away our guns and our bullets. The gun thing isn't about public safety. It's so we can't fight back against them when we the people finally figure out what's going on. The Deep State now has the science to deliver immortality, and it's not about to share it. This is the start of the fucking End Game."

"Who specifically is the *they* you keep talking about? Who are these guys?"

"That's easy. It's the mega wealthy who control the world-wide flow of information. Those arrogant pricks own the search engines, social media sites, battery and computer technology, and effectively, the whole worldwide grid. Dude, they're trillionaires, and through the machines we carry in our pockets, they know everything about us. They control us, and then they buy whatever and whomever they need to do their bidding—including politicians, the media, and the universities."

"I don't know, man. Sounds a little far-fetched to me."

"You think? Hell, you're the one who left the FBI."

"I know. But at the time, I thought it was just dirty politics. This is bigger than that. It's depressing as hell!"

"Sure is. And that's why I'm hoping you have one hell of a plan for when we get to wherever it is your taking us."

"I might. Blue said something about the Three Musketeers coming to a theater near you, and it got me thinking. The only chance we have to come out of this alive is to take our story directly to the people."

"Yeah. Hi, remember me? I'm the nut job who said that the Deep State killed Peanut."

Bennings laughed and said, "Yeah, something like that."

After 10 minutes of silence down the road, Jordan turned to Bennings and asked, "Mind pulling off the road for a minute? I want to grab one of those burner phones you have in the back."

"Sure thing. Who are you calling at this time of night?"

"I wanna check in on Molly. I have a bad feeling all of a sudden."

Bennings nodded, pulled off the side of the

highway, hopped out, and came back with a phone in his hand. He said, "Here, use this. There are four more in back."

"Thanks," Jordan said as he punched in Molly's cell phone number.

On the other end, a man answered and said, "Molly's answering service. Who is it I am speaking to?"

Jordan put his phone on speaker so Bennings could listen and said, "This is Molly's dad. Who the hell is this?"

"Ah, Mr. Nichols. I've been waiting to hear from you. Who I am is not important. What is important is that I've got your daughter, and your mother in my possession. If you don't cooperate, thy will both be dead within 24 hours."

"You son of a bitch, let me speak to Molly—now!"

"Of course. I'd never keep a father from talking with his beloved daughter. Here she is."

"Dad! They came to Nana's house. His name is Willard Lance, and he's..."

Lance yanked the phone out of Molly's hand and said, "Your girl here has a lot of fight in her, but here's the deal. You and Mr. Bennings will deliver Jessie Warring to me in the rear parking lot of Warring Pharmaceuticals at precisely 7 tomorrow night, or little Miss Molly and your mother will both die. It's that simple."

"No, it's not that simple. If you don't let them go right now, I'll take Jessie to the nearest police station, and she will spill her guts about what's been going on out there at the plant. And, in the meantime, if you've done anything to my mother or Molly, you're a dead man. You hear me?"

"You, Mr. Nichols, are not in the position to threaten me. You know, Molly is a very sweet, juicy young woman, and I have a certain affection for her type."

"Why, you piece of shit!"

"Ah Ah. One more disrespectful word out of your mouth, and you'll never see your mother or daughter again. I, on the other hand, will enjoy every inch of Miss Molly here."

Bennings wildly motioned for Jordan to settle down and mouthed the words *I'm dead. Tell him I was killed!*

Jordan bit his lip, took a deep breath and said, "Okay. You're right. I'm sorry. Look, I'll be there with Blue and no games, I promise. But Bennings won't. He died up on that mountain."

"Why should I believe that?"

"I don't know. Just look for his charred remains under the fuselage of the Sikorsky that you or the Deep State sent to kill us. Now tell me exactly what you want me to do!"

"Pull up to the gate at 7 p.m. sharp. The guard will let you in. Proceed around to the back of the warehouse. You give me Jessie. I'll give you Molly and your dear mother. See you then, Mr. Nichols."

Click.

Jordan's head dropped to his chest as Bennings looked over and said, "Sorry, man. Really. I don't know what to say. But I think we just gained the advantage. I know exactly what needs to be done."

Jordan looked up and said, "Yeah, sure…the advantage. But just so you know, I've got no problem trading my life for my daughter's or Blue's. They come first, end of discussion. Promise me you're good with that."

"No. We're all gonna walk away from this alive. That's the only promise you'll get from me."

"Not good enough, bro. If you have to make a choice between any of us tomorrow night, I'm last in line, you hear me?"

"Yeah, sure. I hear you."

Then they drove down the highway in silence.

CHAPTER 30

THE HOTEL'S RADIO at the Holiday Inn Express by the Atlanta Airport clicked on at 6 a.m. Bennings was the first to hear it, maybe because he hadn't slept that well. After getting in around 2 a.m., he had spent the night on the floor, letting Jordan and Blue have the two beds. Bennings staggered to his feet and walked into the bathroom. With a combination of gargle and toothpaste, he won the battle with some bad morning breath.

When he returned to the room, he found Jordan and Blue still sound asleep. He reached to turn off the radio but stopped when he heard the announcer say, "And in other local news, Governor Warring has agreed to an exclusive interview with Bob Asher, CNN's lead political correspondent out of Washington D.C. It will come to you live, straight from the governor's mansion in Milledgeville at 8 tonight. It should be worth listening to. For the first time, she will be revealing the details around all of the key components of her political platform for her run at her party's nomination for President of the United States."

That bitch wants to be on live TV when the news breaks about Blue. That can't be good, Bennings thought.

Bennings shook Jordan out of a deep sleep as he said, "Wake up! Let's go!"

Jordan forced his eyes open, tried to focus, and asked, "What? What time is it?"

"Time to get up. We might have just caught another break."

Jordan flung his legs over the side of the bed, rubbed his hands through his hair, and said, "Go ahead. I'm listening."

"They just announced that Heather Warring has a live interview from the governor's mansion at 8 tonight."

"So?"

"I think she wants the world to learn of our fates during that interview. Given the tight window, it also means that whatever that Lance asshole is planning for you is gonna go down tonight at the plant."

Jordan stood up and as he walked toward the bathroom said, "That's great. Not too many people get to know exactly when, where, and how they're gonna die. Unless, of course, they're on death row."

As the bathroom door started to close, Bennings said, "No. You only know when, where, and how you're *supposed* to die!" After the door shut, Bennings shouted, "Because it's not gonna happen!"

****

Bennings spent the next two hours in the hotel room, picking Blue's brain about every last detail she could provide about the layout of the governor's mansion, Warring's staff, and everything else he could think to ask.

Finally, it was Jordan who said, "That's enough."

Then he turned to Blue and said, "Blue, you've been a big help. Time to hit the road."

Bennings nodded and said, "Tell you what. You two go on ahead without me. I've got some calls to make and people to see so just drop me off at the airport terminal. I'll rent a car. I'll give you the number of my burner phone so if anything comes up, you can call me. Otherwise, I'll see you tonight. When this is all over, the drinks are on me."

Bennings gave Blue a hug, and then he paused, looking Jordan in the eyes before giving him a man hug and saying, "Love ya, brother. It's been a great ride."

Jordan, pulling away, said, "Yeah. Same here."

CHAPTER 31

JORDAN AND BLUE didn't talk much in the car until they reached the exit off of I-20 east onto GA-142, the road leading to Milledgeville. That's when Jordan looked at Blue and asked, "Mind if I take a little detour."

"Where to?"

"To Milledgeville. Bully's Bar and Grill to be exact."

"But what if we're seen?"

"I'll be careful, but when we get close to town, maybe you should scrunch down in back. I'll only be a few minutes."

Blue smiled and asked, "Could it have anything to do with a certain waitress by the name of Kylie?"

"How on earth did you know about that?"

"Mr. Bennings told me. Said he thinks you've got a crush on her. He also said he was really happy for you."

"Yeah. I bet he is."

"No. I could tell, he really meant it."

Then Blue patted Jordan on the shoulder and said, "I'm happy for you, too. It's been a long time."

Jordan slowly nodded and said, "Thanks, Blue."

The conversation triggered a memory for Jordan, and he asked, "By the way, all those years ago, why didn't you go with us to Disney World? It must have stuck in your mind, or you wouldn't have used it for Blue's Code."

Blue laughed and asked. "Is that what you called it, Blue's Code? I like it. Very cool."

Then she turned serious and said, "The only reason I didn't go with you guys was because of my dad. He needed me at home."

"I understand."

****

Twenty minutes later, Jordan punched in a number on his phone. On the other end of the line, he heard Kylie say, "Bully's Bar and Grill. What can I do for you?"

"Kylie, this is Jordan. Can you step outside for a minute? I'm in the Tahoe right in front of the door, and I need to talk to you."

"Are you crazy? Your face is all over the news. You and Bennings are wanted for kidnapping. Jordan, how could you do this?"

"I didn't. That's what I need to talk to you about. Please, trust me."

"No. I never want to see you again, and if you don't leave, I'm calling the police."

While Blue didn't hear everything Kylie had said, she knew it wasn't going well. She popped up from behind the seat and motioned for Jordan to hand her the phone. Jordan hesitated, but Blue grabbed it out of his hand and said, "Kylie, this is Jessie Warring. Please just look out the window. Jordan didn't kidnap me; he's trying to save me. Come out here, and I'll explain everything."

Kylie's face turned white. She nervously set the phone down and walked toward the window. When she saw Jessie wave, she ran back to the phone, hung it up, and called out, "Ducky, I'll be right back. I have to run outside for a minute."

When she approached the car, Jordan reached across, pushed the passenger's door open, and said, "Please?" Kylie tentatively sat down in the passenger's seat and pulled the door shut.

Blue was the first to speak, saying, "Hi, Kylie. I know this seems weird, but last week, did you see the news about how I was almost killed in the parking lot at the Varsity?"

Kylie nodded and said, "Yeah. I'm so sorry about your friend."

"Well my mother was behind that. I'm positive, and that's why Jordan and Mr. Bennings figured out a way to get me away from her."

Kylie got a flustered look on her face and said, "I don't know. This is all beyond me." Then she saw the blood soaking through Jordan's shirt and said, "Oh my God, you're hurt."

Jordan took her hand, smiled and said, "It's okay. All that matters right now is that you shouldn't believe what you're hearing on the news. Jessie and I go way back. She reached out to me to help her get away from Heather Warring, and that's why Bennings and I came down here in the first place."

"But then why are you here now? You should be long gone. Half the world is looking for you."

"I know. But I wanted you to hear the truth—in person. That's all."

Jordan reached across with his left hand and

pushed open the door. Kylie grabbed his forearm, hesitated, and then said, "You two be careful, you hear?"

Jordan smiled and said, "We'll do our best."

Kylie got out and closed the door. Jordan backed up, turned, and pulled out of the lot.

CHAPTER 32

IT WAS ONLY 10 minutes before 7 when Jordan's phone rang.

It was Bennings asking, "Where are you guys?"

"We're almost there. Why didn't you answer any of my earlier calls?"

"Sorry, I had a lot goin' on, but listen up. I'm pretty sure Molly's inside Warring's labs and your mom's with her. They're both still alive."

"Thank God. How do you know for sure?"

"I asked a friend of mine to do some surveillance out there earlier today. He saw both of them being taken into the building. My guess, they're up on the second floor in one of those cells."

"Where are you now?"

"I'm about 20 minutes out, so stall as long as you can."

"Sure, why not. I'm in no hurry to die."

"Figured as much."

"Bennings, if this doesn't go down according to plan, remember, job one is to protect my family. I'm expendable."

Click. The phone went dead.

Jessie looked at him and asked, "What did you mean by that?"

Jordan pulled the Tahoe off the road and put it in park as Blue looked at him and repeated the question, "I asked what you meant by that—that you're expendable!"

Jordan said, "Okay, time to talk. I want to tell you how much it's meant to me to finally see you again, to spend some time together after all these years. This has been one hell of an adventure. Wouldn't you agree?"

"Okay I guess, but this is gonna turn out alright, isn't it? Mr. Bennings told me that he has it all figured out!"

Jordan said, "Look, no matter what happens, no regrets—for either of us. My wife's death forced me to look at things a little differently. I realized that life can't be measured by how long we live. It can only be measured by how we live in those precious moments of time that God gives us. To spend the past few weeks with you, trying to save the world, well hey..." Jordan paused, fighting his emotions. Then he said, "Blue, it's been an honor. It really has."

A tear running down her cheek, Blue gave Jordan a peck on the cheek, forced a smile, and said, "Now stop it. Mr. Bennings has got this under control. I just know it!"

Jordan nodded, put the truck back in drive, and said, "Okay. Then, let's go get this thing over with."

A mile down the road, Jordan pulled the Tahoe into the parking lot at Warring Pharmaceuticals and paused, 30 yards from the guardhouse. A full moon, dancing in and out from behind the clouds, bounced moonlight off the razor wire atop the fence, reminding Jordan just how much the complex looked like a prison. He noticed that the parking lot was abandoned, and that all the lights had been turned off. He looked at Blue, said, "Here we go," and pulled up to the guardhouse as he rolled down the window.

The guard leaned out of the guardhouse, scanned the inside of the Tahoe, and said, "You're late. They're waiting for you around back."

Jordan nodded and slowly moved forward. Fifteen feet short of the rear corner of the building a tall man, dressed in black, moved out of the shadows, startling Jordan. He pointed a semi-automatic rifle toward the truck, making sure Jordan took notice.

Nice gun. A short-nosed Honey Badger with a silencer! Jordan thought.

The man motioned for Jordan to stop and roll down the window. He peered inside, glanced at Blue, and then turned his attention to Jordan and said, "Turn off your headlights and move around back. When you turn the corner, pull up to the loading dock, shut off the engine, and toss the keys out the window."

Jordan nodded and said, "Whatever you say, boss."

The man walked alongside of the Tahoe as they moved forward. Jordan, looking straight ahead quietly said, "Blue, when we come to a stop, you stay inside. When I hop out, lock the doors, and do not open them unless I say so. We need to buy a little more time for Bennings. Remember, my Glock is right in front of you, inside the glove box, just like we talked about. There's a round in the chamber and it's got a trigger safety. What that means is if you need it, just point the gun and pull the trigger. You've got 16 shots."

When they got near the loading dock, the man signaled Jordan to stop. Jordan put the truck in park, turned off the ignition, and hopped out.

Jordan dangled the keys in front of the man, tossed them as far as he could, and said, "Here, rover, go fetch."

"Why, you son of a bitch" yelled the man as he slammed the butt of his rifle into Jordan's bad shoulder. Jordan screamed in pain and fell to his knees. Inside the Tahoe, Blue scrambled to pull the gun out of the glove box as she watched the man point the rifle at Jordan and say, "I'd like to…"

As Blue was about to pull the trigger, a voice yelled out, "No! Not yet, Ricky! Just go find the damn keys. I'll take it from here." As Ricky lowered his rifle, Willard Lance walked out from the shadows. With him was a mean looking woman, covered in tattoos, armed with a Honey Badger.

Lance directed the woman toward Jordan, saying, "Search him," as Lance moved toward the passenger's door of the Tahoe. Blue quickly set the gun inside of the glove box but didn't have a chance to close it before Lance glanced in, pulled on the door handle and said, "Now Jessie, you're not gonna make me play some childish little game here, are you? Open the damn door."

Not getting a response, Lance called out into the darkness, "Hey, Ricky, you find those keys yet?"

"Nope."

"Then come back here and shoot the damn lock off the door."

Jordan staggered to his feet and said, "Wait!

Don't bother. Blue, open the door." Blue unlocked the car door, and then grabbed for the gun, but Lance was too quick. He pushed past her and slammed the glove box on her hand, holding it tight. As she winced in pain, Lance said, "Now let go of that gun and play nice, okay, Jessie?"

She dropped the gun and Lance eased the pressure, letting her pull her hand out. Then he grabbed her by the hair and yanked her out of the truck. After slamming the truck door shut, Lance shoved Blue in Jordan's direction and said, "Okay, now both of you, move to the wall."

Jordan said, "No! Not until I see Molly. That was the deal. I get Molly. You get Jessie."

An arrogant smirk crossed Lance's face as he said, "Mr. Nichols. You're a smart man. Did you really think that was gonna happen?"

"Why not? It's a fair trade. You kill me and blame it on Bennings as a kidnapping gone bad. The girls won't talk. Why would they? I'll be dead, and they can live the rest of their lives knowing that if they do, you'll hunt them down and kill them. Everybody wins."

Blue cried out, "If you kill Mr. Nichols, I'll… I'll…"

Lance burst out laughing. "What? You'll tell your mommy?"

Blue started to cry as Lance turned to Jordan and said, "You see, the deal is you showed up here to pick up a $2 million ransom, and Bennings double-crossed you. He killed you and Jessie and then took off with the money. I've already got a record for the funds withdrawal, and a nicely doctored re-cording of a phone call from you to me, telling me where to meet you with the ransom money."

"But what about Molly and my mother? How are you gonna explain that away?"

"Oh, yes. Glad you reminded me. It seems that the two of them are gonna be so heartbroken that they take their own lives. Molly's already written a nice little suicide note for me. She was very cooper-ative after I told her it would save your life. Oh, and they'll be found at your parents' place, right after the news of your death hits the wire. Now...up against the wall!

Over your dead body, mother fucker. Come on, Ben-nings. We're running out of time, Jordan thought.

As Jordan and Blue were being shoved toward the back wall of the building, Bennings was 70 yards away, just outside the chain link fence surrounding the perimeter. He rested the barrel of his scoped Remington 700 on the fence as he drew a bead. The first to die would be the woman. She was pointing her rifle at Blue, and Bennings was going to keep his promise. At the sound of the shot, Jordan would turn on the guard closest to him and, if things went as planned, it would give Bennings the time for a second, maybe even a third clean shot before anyone could take cover.

Bennings had already released the safety and moved his finger to the trigger when, *click*, he heard the hammer of a revolver being pulled back. He tried to free the rifle from the fence, but it was too late. He felt the barrel of a gun at the back of his head, and then he heard the words, "Drop it, and step away."

Fuck! How could I be so stupid?

Bennings dropped his rifle and slowly stood up and turned. The man facing him was the security guard from the front gate, and he had his .38 special trained on Bennings. The guard backed away, held the gun on him with one hand, and used the other to push the call button on a walkie-talkie and say, "You were right, Mr. Lance. I got him."

"Very good. Bring him down here. I'll wait."

Lance smiled at Jordan and said, "What do you know! Bennings is alive after all. Who woulda thought?"

"Fuck you!"

Lance punched Jordan in his bad shoulder, and he, once again, fell to the ground in pain. Blue, sobbing, screamed, "Will you just leave him alone? Please, I'm begging you!"

Lance grabbed Blue's hair, yanked it away from her ear, and whispered, "You're begging me? Well guess what? Your friend Peanut begged me too. When I was screwing her and guess what else, bitch, your mother didn't care. She knew all about it. Stop with the begging, or you'll get the same thing that Peanut got."

Blue turned and spit in Lance's face. A split second later, hit her as hard as he could, back-handed. She fell to the ground next to Jordan as Lance walked away.

With the two guards standing over them, Jordan looked at Blue and asked, "You okay?"

Blue, sobbing, said, "I think so."

A minute later, the guard arrived with Bennings and asked Lance, "Where do you want him?"

Lance pointed to the ground next to Jordan and

said, "Throw him down there with the others for now. I need to rethink how we can stage this thing now that Bennings showed up."

The guard shoved Bennings in the back and said, "You heard the man, down on the ground. Put your arms above your head."

Bennings said, "Okay, asshole. Chill."

As Bennings got down on the ground next to Jordan he said, "Sorry. I really fucked this thing up. Looks like our only option is to charge these guys and take our chances. Maybe one of us lives."

Jordan said, "Okay. But I make the first move, and you follow. The second guy has to be quick— able to react. That's not me, not with this shoulder."

"Agreed. Let Blue know. For the record, it's been fun."

"Yeah, a real blast."

Jordan turned his head toward Blue and said, "Blue, when we make a move, you stay put. Stay flat on the ground until you see an opening and then you get up run as fast as you can into the dark. No matter what you hear, just keep running. No arguments. Understood?"

"Yes, sir."

Jordan rose to one knee as he called out, "Hey! What the hell are you guys doing over there, planning the senior prom? My shoulder is killing me, so can we please just get this thing over with."

Lance glared at him and said, "Really, your shoulder hurts?" Then he nodded at Ricky and said, "Why don't you show Mr. Nichols what real pain feels like."

Ricky smiled and walked toward Jordan, pulling

back his Honey Badger to slam the stock into Jordan's shoulder.

Jordan was about to make his move when *BANG*—a rifle shot rang out from somewhere beyond the perimeter. Jordan was the first to realize what had happened. He had been looking directly into Ricky's eyes when they bugged out, his face contorting from the impact of a high-powered round hitting him square in the forehead. The force threw his body backward onto the pavement, with blood quickly starting to pool around the exit wound in the back of his skull.

Bennings was quick to react. He sprung to his feet and lunged at the woman, who was standing less than five feet away. Bennings hit her chest to chest, knocking both of them to the ground as the Honey Badger fell from her hands. Bennings quickly maneuvered behind her, putting a lethal chokehold around her neck while using his legs to control her like a wrestler throwing in a crab ride. The guard with the .38 special turned to fire at Bennings but hesitated, waiting for a clean shot.

BANG! It cost him his life.

He fell to the ground with a bullet in the back of his head, fired from the same rifle that had taken out Ricky seconds earlier.

As that shot was being fired, Jordan charged Lance.

This is really gonna hurt. Jordan landed on top of him as they both crashed to the pavement. With Jordan crying out in pain, Lance quickly rolled out from under and sunk the ball of his hand deep into Jordan's bad shoulder.

As Jordan started to lose consciousness, Lance smiled and asked, "Hurts, doesn't it?" Then he reached behind his back and pulled a 9 mm pistol from his belt. He jumped up, straddled Jordan with his feet, and lined up a kill shot when *BANG*—a close range pistol shot rang out.

The gun dropped from Lance's hand, and he staggered backward. He turned to his right to see Blue standing by the Tahoe pointing Jordan's gun at him. Then he looked down to see blood filling the front of his pants in the crotch area as Blue said, "That one was for Peanut, you son of a bitch."

Then *BANG!* She shot him again, this time in the chest. As he fell to the ground dead, she said, "That one was for me."

Jordan, semi-conscious, looked up to see Blue leaning down and asking, "Are you alright?"

Jordan offered up a weak smile and said, "Not again?"

Jordan staggered to his feet and turned his attention toward Bennings, just in time to see him release his chokehold. As the woman slumped to the pavement, Jordan knew she was dead. He knew first-hand about Bennings's martial arts skills.

The three of them looked at each other for a few seconds, the smallest smiles of relief showing on their faces, and then Jordan asked, "What? Who?"

Bennings said, "I don't know. But right now, we need to get inside the building, or it won't matter."

Jordan said, "Roger that." And they quickly moved toward the rear entrance.

Bennings stopped and said, "Wait a minute, forgot something."

He ran over to Lance's body and pulled out his wallet. A second later, he pulled a key card out of the wallet and said, "This oughta open some doors."

CHAPTER 33

AS BENNINGS WAS using Lance's security card to open the door by the loading dock, the three of them heard sirens approaching. They exchanged glances and then quickly moved inside. They sprinted down the hall, past the kitchen and took a right turn to another hallway. Bennings pointed to the scanner on the wall and said, "There it is!"

The three of them pulled up. Jordan looked at Bennings and asked, "Now what? Schulman used that thing to scan his eyeball."

Bennings said, "Let's hope this card works. Otherwise, I'll have to go back outside and pop Lance's eyeball out of his skull."

Bennings held the key card up and waved it in front of the scanner. A second later, the wall panel opened as Bennings smiled and Blue said, "Thank God."

They jumped in the elevator and when they reached the second floor, Bennings and Jordan sprinted to the solid metal door as Blue followed behind. Bennings waved Lance's card, and the door lock released. With Blue waiting by the door, Bennings and Jordan rushed down the corridor as Jordan yelled "Molly! Mom! Can you hear me?

Nervous seconds of silence followed until, halfway down the hallway, they heard a muffled, "Dad! We're in here!"

Jordan charged ahead of Bennings, yelling, "Keep talking. Where are you?" As he neared the center of the corridor, he heard, "We're in here. In here!"

He stopped in front of one of the service doors, the same kind they pried open on their past visit, and Bennings waved Lance's key card across the electric eye. The door's lock released. When Jordan raised the door, he found Molly waiting for him on the other side. Barbara, his mother, was lying on a nearby couch, her head wrapped in a bloody bandage. Jordan reached his arm down through the opening, taking Molly's hand as she said, "Dad, you've got to get us out. Nana's not doing so well. They cracked her head with a rifle butt when she wouldn't go in the cell."

Jordan said, "Okay. I'll be there in a couple of minutes. Can you remember anything about how they got you in there?"

"Yes. Just go to the end of the hall you're in and turn right. You go down some steps and then there's another door on your right that gets you to the front of these cells. Dad, there's a whole bunch of other people in here. Most of them are women!"

"I know. I'll be there real soon. Now go help your Nana."

Jordan turned to Bennings and said, "I need to get to Molly right away."

Bennings nodded and said, "Take the key card. I need to stall the cops until Keaster gets here."

Jordan said, "Keaster?"

"That was one of my stops today. Like Blue said, 'We had to bring this show to a theater near you.'"

"Okay. Then keep her with you. She can probably help with the cops. See you in a couple of minutes."

Jordan took the key card, and they split up. No sooner had Bennings retraced his steps and got to Blue when the two of them heard a voice on a megaphone from outside the building, back by the loading dock.

"Jordan Nichols, William Bennings. We know you are in there, and the building is surrounded. Make it easy for all of us and come out with your hands in the air. If you don't cooperate, we will have no choice but to take you by force."

Bennings pulled out his burner phone and punched in a number. On the other end he heard Keaster's voice say, "Is this Bennings?"

"Who else? You here yet?"

"Yeah, I'm here. But I'm looking at four dead people, and that was never part of the deal."

"Listen, those dead people are the bad guys. Tell the police that if they let you and your camera crew in here for 10 minutes, we will surrender and come out with our hands up. If they don't, we're gonna hole up in here and start killing off hostages. You are the only one we want to communicate with."

A minute later, Bennings's cell phone rang. It was Keaster who said, "The police have the logbook from the guard house outside, and they say there's no one in there with you."

Next a different voice said, "That's right, Mr. Bennings. This is Officer Daughtry of the Georgia state police. We don't believe that anyone else is in there. You've got exactly two minutes to walk out here with your hands up, or we're coming in with our guns up."

Blue, listening in on the conversation, ripped the phone from Bennings and said, "Officer Daughtry, this is Jessie Warring. Did you forget about me? If you don't do as Bennings says, they say they're gonna kill me. Do you want to have to explain that to my mother?" Blue hung up as Bennings smiled in appreciation.

A minute later, Officer Daughtry, this time back on the bullhorn said, "Okay. We have Keaster and his camera crew waiting by the back entrance. We'll back off and give you five minutes, but that's all. Then we're coming in."

Bennings looked at Blue and said, "Come on, let's move. You're gonna have to hold the elevator open on the first floor for me while I go for Keaster."

Blue said, "Okay. But first, I need to make a call."

"To who?"

"A close friend."

Bennings nodded and took off for the loading dock door. By the time he got there, Jordan had already worked his way to the door that Molly had said would give him access to the front side of the cellblock. He used Lance's key card, waived it over the electronic eye, and heard the click. When he walked through the door, he wasn't prepared for what he saw.

CHAPTER 34

HEATHER WARRING'S PRIME time interview with Bob Asher, GNN's anchor from the Washington desk, was about to wrap up when they went to commercial break. Asher smiled at Warring and said, "Nice job. You have my vote."

Warring returned the smile and said, "Why thank you so much. I look forward to working with you once I get settled in up there."

Behind the two cameras being used, Travis stood off to the side. He was on a cell phone and said, "Will do. You just be careful." Then, he hung up. He walked up toward one of the cameramen and started motioning wildly toward Heather Warring.

She saw him, then turned to Asher and said, "Excuse me, I'll be right back," and stood up, disconnected her microphone from the battery pack, and set it down on the chair.

Asher said, "Governor, you have 45 seconds."

Warring nodded as she walked over to Travis and said, "What is it Travis? Is there a call for me?"

"No. But Mr. Lance just called me. He said that it was urgent. I'm supposed to tell you that it all went as planned and that you'd understand."

Warring didn't show any emotion until she turned away and walked slowly back toward Asher.

Then her lip started to quiver. By the time she sat down and reconnected her microphone, a tear had appeared in her eye.

Behind the camera, a voice said "four, three, two, one, and..."

When the camera turned on, Asher found himself looking at Governor Warring as she started to sob. He had no choice but to ask, "What is it, Governor? What's wrong?"

Heather Warring looked directly into the camera and said, "I've just been told that they've found my Jessie, and that...that she's...that she's been murdered by the kidnappers."

Asher said, "Oh my God, I am so sorry. Please," and turning toward the camera he continued, "Take the camera off the governor and pull in on me. America, this is tragic. We need to go back to the studio now so Governor Warring can deal with this in privacy. Washington, take over for now. As for the rest of us, let us all pray for Governor Warring."

As the Washington news desk took over for all of GNN's affiliates, there was a frantic discussion going on at Atlanta's news desk. The man in charge that night was Fred Hutchins, and he was on the phone with Brent Keaster.

Keaster yelled at him, "Take me live. Now! I am at Warring Pharmaceuticals. I'm right in the middle of the biggest news story of our lifetime."

Hutchins said, "I can't do that. Jessie Warring has just been found murdered, and I've got orders to stay plugged into the Washington office. They're coordinating all coverage."

Keaster said, "Well, I'm standing right beside

Jessie Warring, and she sure as hell doesn't look dead to me."

Phones were ringing off the hook around Hutchins. Having just been promoted to assistant news director, he was in over his head. Panicked, he said, "I don't know. I've got orders from…"

Keaster interrupted, saying, "Just cut to me, you idiot. Last time I looked, I was still the news anchor in Atlanta. If I'm wrong, I'll take all the heat."

Hutchins, his eyes on a monitor said, "Okay, Washington just went to commercial break. I can give you at least the next two minutes."

For viewers in the Atlanta market, their televisions suddenly flipped from a commercial out of the Washington desk to a live news feed from Atlanta where Brent Keaster was standing next to Jessie Warring.

"This is Brent Keaster, and I'm standing here live with Jessie Warring, Heather Warring's daughter. Jessie, your mother just told the world that you'd been murdered. What do you have to say to that?"

"That my mother is a complete fraud. She tried to have me murdered and frame Jordan Nichols and William Bennings. These men didn't kidnap me. They rescued me from her! When you see what's going on here inside of Warring Pharmaceuticals, you'll understand why. Now, please follow me into the secret lab that she's been operating."

Blue walked ahead of the camera crew as viewers followed a bouncing picture being transmitted by a cameraman with a shoulder-mounted camera as he tried to keep up. Halfway down the hall, Blue slowed her pace, allowing Keaster to catch up with his microphone. Then she turned and said, "There really is a Deep State, and they just tried to kill all of us up on top of a mountain in North Carolina. Check news accounts for the helicopter that crashed up there. Mr. Bennings, a former FBI agent, shot it down because they were using it to launch killer drones at us."

Blue turned the corner at the end of the corridor, again with the camera crew and Kester in tow, and paused by the doorway leading to the cells. She looked into the camera and said, "Now, you're about to see the cells where my mother keeps prisoners, most of them kidnapped from WWA foster homes, for human experiments." She opened the door and paused in front of the first cell, allowing the cameraman to scan the area. It didn't have any bars. It was made of a thick, clear acrylic material. Inside was what appeared to be an 85-year-old woman, huddled in a corner with a blanket pulled around her. Blue motioned to the cameraman and said, "Look! Point the camera in there." Then she pointed to a chart that was on the door and said, "Then focus in on the chart. The Deep State and my mother are doing stem cell research on human beings... not to find cures for failing organs, but to try to reverse the aging process! See for yourself!"

On the chart was the following information:

Patient's Name:	Chrissy Malcolm
Age at beginning of trial:	15 years, three months
Case start Date:	03/25/22
Case Objective:	Advance to 80 years old and stabilize
Case Reference #	143-67A

Keaster asked Blue, "Are you telling me that secret human trials are going on here? Something to do with the aging process?"

Jessie said, "Pretty sure that's what I just said! Now, follow me to this next cell."

The television audience watched as the cameraman followed her down the hall to a cell holding what appeared to be a teenager. Her chart read:

Patient's Name:	Stacy Whitlock
Age at beginning of trial:	45 years, seven months
Case start Date:	06/05/22
Case Objective:	Revert to 14 years old and then monitor for resumption of aging
Case Reference #	162-62B

Jessie said, "See... This is what they've been working on. They've cracked the code to immortality, right here in my mother's labs. And when I found out, they decided to kill me."

Keaster shook his head and said, "No. This simply can't be."

Bennings and Jordan walked out of the cell three spaces down, Jordan still holding his 9mm Glock. When Keaster saw the gun, he quickly backed away, moving out of camera view. Jordan, seeing the reaction said, "Sorry, no worries," and laid the gun on the ground. When Keaster moved forward with the microphone, Jordan took it out of his hand and, looking into the camera said, "Come here. I want you to meet someone by the name of Stacy. I'd like her to tell you her story." He waved the key card in front of the cell's sensor, heard the release and walked in as Keaster, his cameraman, and Bennings followed behind. Jordan, still holding the microphone, sat down next to the girl and said, "Hi, Stacy, how are you doing?"

Showing no emotion, she said, "Like I just told you, I'll be doing a lot better when you let me out of here."

Jordan said, "I know. But first, why don't you look into that camera and tell the people what you just told me a few minutes ago."

Stacy nodded and said, "Sure. I'm 45 years old and a year ago, I was homeless...that is until I was kidnapped off the streets of Atlanta and thrown in here. They started injecting me with all sorts of things and in all sorts of different places. So now look at me. They tell me I'm about 15 years old again. I don't mind that part, but I sure don't want to stay in here the rest of my life."

Jordan, turning to Keaster said, "A few more cells down the hall, you'll find my daughter and my mother. Warring's head of security, one of the dead men lying outside of this building, kidnapped them and brought them here to force Bennings and I to surrender Jessie. The plan was to murder all of us, calling it a kidnapping gone bad. Oh, and back in the labs, near the elevator, you'll find the machine they've been using to dispose of all the dead bodies they've been racking up. Please believe me. The Deep State is real, and its real name is the Guild. Half of the politicians in Washington D.C., along with all the wealthiest people in the world, are part of it. If we the people don't revolt soon, we will no longer be free. In fact, most of us will probably be dead. Their long-term plans do not include us. The earth cannot sustain a population that is immortal, and that is precisely why they have tried to ruin our economy, turn us against each other, and to expose us to diseases for which they have developed their own private immunizations. If we don't fight back soon, it will be too late."

As Jordan was handing the microphone back to Keaster, Officer Daughtry and five other state troopers in S.W.A.T gear could be heard outside the cell, storming down the hall. Bennings and Jordan, familiar with the procedure, quickly assumed the position against the cell wall. Seconds later, one of the S.W.A.T. team frisked them as Officer Daughtry, looking on from the doorway pulled out his walkie-talkie and said, "We're gonna need a lot of assistance in here. No, not armed backup. I'm talking Health and Human Services. I've never seen anything like this."

CHAPTER 35

THE ATLANTA DESK had stayed with the coverage inside of Warring, even though it would soon cost both Fred Hutchins, and Brent Keaster their jobs. But Heather Warring hadn't seen any of it. As soon as the cameras inside the mansion were turned off, she had excused herself and retreated into her private living quarters. Alone, she broke out her favorite cognac and basked in the glow of a great interview as well as the resolution of the problems caused by her insolent adopted daughter.

Then her phone rang. It wasn't the ring tone reserved for commoners. By the ring, she knew it was a member of the Guild, one that had been routed through the encryption software.

"Yes! Heather Warring speaking."

"Good evening, Heather. How are you this evening?"

Heather could hardly contain her excitement.

Oh my God. It's the former President.

"I'm good Mr. President. Did you happen to catch my interview with CNN?"

"I certainly did. I especially enjoyed the performance regarding the loss of your daughter."

Performance? How did he know? What's this all about?

"Well, uh, thank you. I thought it went very well."

"Oh, it certainly did. But if I were you, I'd turn on the TV. Seems that you've become the subject of an awful lot of discussion tonight."

"Oh, thank you, I certainly…"

Click The phone went dead.

Heather pushed an intercom button next to her chair and said, "Travis."

There was no response. She tried it again and again, still no response.

Damn it, I'll turn it on for myself.

Heather Warring stood up and walked toward the TV set. She never got there. As she passed by the window, six drones were hovering outside. None of them missed their mark.

EPILOGUE

ONE WEEK LATER

BENNINGS AND JORDAN were sitting across from each other in Bully's, watching as Kylie set an order of hotcakes with a side of bacon down in front of Jordan and said, "Here you go, sweetie."

She turned to Bennings and asked, "You sure I can't get you anything?"

Bennings smiled and said, "No, thanks. This coffee is all I need. Unlike my friend here, I need to lose a couple of pounds. This Southern cooking's not good for the waistline."

Kylie said, "I hear ya! But after you smell those delicious hotcakes, I'll bet you change your mind!"

As Kylie turned to leave, Jordan gently touched her arm and said, "We're still on for tonight, aren't we?"

Kylie smiled and said, "You bet."

"Good. See you at 6."

Bennings laughed and said, "I knew it. You two. I just knew it."

Jordan smiled and said, "Shut up and drink your coffee."

Kylie laughed and said, "Yeah, you just be quiet now, you hear?"

Bennings laughed again and said, "Yes ma'am."

After Kylie left, Bennings said, "I'm happy for you, Jordan. I really am. Does this mean you'll be staying down here for a while?"

"Too early to tell, but I sure hope so. Molly and Blue are with my mom up in New York, for now, so who knows. Besides, I'd still like to find whoever it was that saved our asses last week. I'd like to thank him."

Bennings said, "You sure? Given the grilling they're putting us through, don't you think it's for the best that we don't know who it was?"

"Maybe so."

Bennings, looking out in the parking lot, watched Taylor Riggs get out of his truck, enter the restaurant, and sit down at the counter. It didn't go unnoticed. When Bennings turned his attention back to Jordan, Jordan smiled and said, "You think it was Riggs. Don't you?"

"Maybe. After all, he helped us more than once over the past couple of weeks. He's also the guy who saw Lance take Molly and your mom inside."

"Really? You never told me that."

"You never asked. Anyway, on a different subject, I wanted you to know that I'm thinking of moving out of the country. Maybe finding a little shack down in Aruba or Barbados."

"Really! I never pictured you as the type who can just lie on a beach nursing a bottle of rum."

"Maybe not. But this thing isn't going away anytime soon."

Jordan nodded and said, "Yeah, I know. Look at how they took out Warring last week."

"No shit. That was meant as a show of power and, I figure we're next in line. That's why I'm going off the grid for awhile. I think you should join me."

"No thanks. I still think our only chance is a revolution by and for the people. We need to find a warrior leader, a modern-day version of George Washington."

"It won't work. Two hundred and fifty years ago, we could see the whites of their eyes. Today, there's no visible enemy, and that same enemy controls all communications. We'll never be able to rally the troops. Especially not in the pussified, politically correct world we're living in."

"But it was the Deep State that created this pussified, politically correct world! They've systematically ripped the balls off of every college kid by feeding them bullshit ideas like politically correct and white privilege... for the sole purpose of eliminating freedom of speech, our right to congregate, and our ability to think for ourselves."

Bennings took a sip of coffee and said, "Yup, and guess what? It worked. Hell, you and I have already done more than our part. You even made your case on national TV. And what did it get us? The media turned around and painted Warring as a lone wolf eccentric seeking the fountain of youth. And then they chalked up her assassination as being carried out by the same right wing extremist group that tried to take out Blue at The Varsity. The people actually believe that shit. The bad guys win; we lose. End of discussion."

They sat in silence for a few minutes until Bennings pointed toward the counter and said, "But if you're still a believer, Riggs over there has an interesting past."

"How's that?"

"When he was serving in Iraq, one day the bad guys brought down one of our choppers—an Apache. They were moving in for the kill when Riggs took up a position on a nearby sand dune and took out an entire platoon single-handed, taking two rounds to the gut in the process. He saved the day and earned himself a Medal of Honor."

"Very impressive. How did he pull that off?"

Bennings smiled and asked, "Didn't I tell you? He was a sniper."

"You son of a bitch! You've known all along it was him out there. Why didn't you tell me before?"

"Like I said, thought it best you didn't know."

"And now?"

"Because you just told me you were looking for a warrior leader, a modern-day George Washington."

Jordan glanced over at the counter and saw Riggs standing up to leave. He called out to him, "Hey, Taylor, got a minute? I'd like to talk to you about something."

Bennings shook his head and smiled.

Here we go again!

THE END

Made in the USA
Columbia, SC
28 May 2022